A PLACE OF BELONGING

A Place of Belonging

Five Founding Women of Fairbanks, Alaska

Phyllis Demuth Movius

University of Alaska Press
Fairbanks

Copyright © 2009 University of Alaska Press
P.O. Box 756240
Fairbanks, AK 99775-6240

second printing 2011

This publication was printed on paper that meets the minimum requirements
for ANSI/NISO Z39.48-1992 (Permanence of Paper).

Library of Congress Cataloging-in-Publication Data

Movius, Phyllis Demuth.
A place of belonging : five founding women of Fairbanks, Alaska / Phyllis Movius.
p. cm.
ISBN 978-1-60223-064-4 (cloth : alk. paper)
1. Women pioneers—Alaska—Fairbanks—Biography. 2. Women—Alaska—
Fairbanks—Biography. 3. Fairbanks (Alaska)—Biography. 4. Women—
Alaska—Fairbanks—Social life and customs—20th century. 5. Fairbanks
(Alaska)—Social life and customs—20th century. 6. Fairbanks (Alaska)—
History—20th century. I. Title.
F914.F16M68 2009
979.8'030922—dc22
[B]
2009009858

Cover design by Dixon Jones, Rasmuson Library Graphics
Interior design by Rebecca Hurbi

Contents

List of Abbreviations

AJAC   American Jewish Archives Collection
CFHR   City of Fairbanks Historical Records
RFP   Rust Family Papers
FEWML Frances E. Willard Memorial Library
HFP   Harrais Family Papers
RJBP   Robert and Jessie Bloom Papers
SEGC   Sarah Ellen Gibson Collection

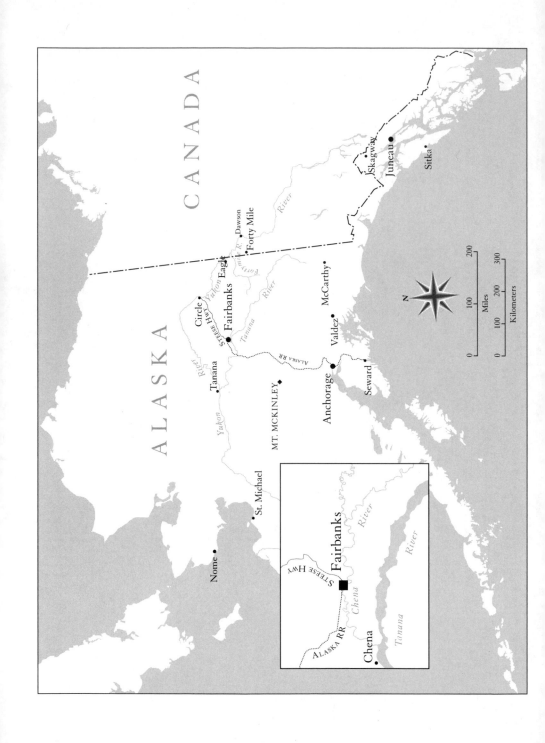

Preface

INSPIRED BY MY OWN recreational wilderness experiences living in a cabin on the Goodpaster River in the Big Delta region of Alaska's Interior, my research about how women lived in the early days of Fairbanks was initiated by simple curiosity. Introduction to the ever-growing body of literature about women on America's western frontier deepened my interest in Alaska's pioneer women, and I began to apply the questions asked about women in the West to women in the North. What preconceptions did women have about Alaska's wilderness and its Native population? Were these ideas changed by life on the new frontier? What social, economic, cultural, and intellectual preparation did women have for the new experience in the North? Were adaptations made to their previously held ideals of woman's place in the home and in society? Did women assume new roles as a result of their pioneering experience, and did these changes affect individual and national perceptions of woman's place? In what ways did women's impressions of and adaptations to life on an isolated frontier differ from men's?

Though many residents and nonresidents still like to think of Alaska as the "last frontier"—and indeed the phrase is the state slogan—Alaska historian Stephen Haycox has pointed out that today "there is little in Alaska that resembles frontier settlement."[1] Seventy percent of Alaskans live in the state's urban centers, which are replete with all the technology and conveniences contained in the "Lower 48"—the term Alaskans use to describe the forty-eight contiguous United States. Haycox mused, "Alaska has not evolved in a vacuum."[2] Even though, from the onset of American settlement of Alaska, the federal government and private corporations have pumped in a continuous stream of money to establish jobs and an economic base to encourage settlement, early pioneering efforts required sacrifice and daring. Alaskans may no longer be considerered exceptional because of where they live, but certainly the early settlers can be credited with doing something bold and adventurous.[3]

Alaska has always attracted a diverse group of women and men from varied backgrounds for a variety of reasons. The women presented in this book are examples of a disparate population that has long enriched Alaska and continues to attract people to the North. This book explores the lives of women who settled in Fairbanks between 1903 and 1923, prior to the opening of the Alaska Railroad and the advent of big mining. It provides insight into their motivations, resource-fulness, and accomplishments. The quality of women's daily lives is represented by biographical portraits of five women. Their stories were woven together from the women's own recollections preserved in letters, memoirs, personal papers, club records, and, to a limited degree, their oral histories and published writ-ings. As such, the quantity of available material dictated which women could be included. The women represented here came from a variety of backgrounds, education, and experiences. They left behind personal documentation of their lives, shaping a perspective of Fairbanks history with their grit, determination, trials, and victories. Information about the lives of many other women who participated in the early development of Fairbanks is not as accessible—their memoirs may be embedded in less definable oral histories or other individuals' stories and recollections. Their part in the broad examination of women's his-torical roles awaits discovery and analysis.

Acknowledgments

THERE ARE MANY individuals to whom I am indebted for their assistance with this project. I am grateful to all of the archive, library, and historical society staff who responded to my requests. However, some stand out for their willingness to go beyond what is expected. Meta Bloom Buttnick's many letters provided perspective from otherwise elusive information that added depth to the chapters about her mother, Jessie Bloom, and their family friends, Mary Lee Davis and Aline Baskerville Bradley Beegler. Considerable assistance with the biographical portrait of Mary Lee came from Jean N. Berry, Archives Assistant at the Margaret Clapp Library of Wellesley College, and Nanci A. Young, Assistant Archivist at the Seeley G. Mudd Manuscript Library of Princeton University, who put me in touch with Mary Lee's sister-in-law, Joyce Cadwell Lewis. Mrs. Lewis is especially appreciated for generously sharing information from family records. When Signe J. Kelker of the Ezra Lehman Memorial Library at Shippensburg University began his search for material related to Mary Lee's mother a steady stream of manuscript material and microfilm were forthcoming. Contact with Kay Ackerman, Archivist and Assistant Professor of History at the C. Elizabeth Boyd Archival Center of Wilson College, provided additional information about Mary Lee's mother, and Frank K. Lorenz, Curator of Special Collections at Hamilton College, was instrumental with assistance about Mary Lee's father.

Alfred Epstein of the Frances E. Willard Memorial Library of the Woman's Christian Temperance Union in Evanston, Illinois, worked tirelessly to supply documents related to Margaret Keenan Harrais's work with the organization. Through his dedication, I was able to focus on this little known facet of her life. Noble County, Ohio, genealogist and historian Lois Blake wrote that the search for information about Margaret's ancestry "has been one of the ones I have most enjoyed doing in the twenty-five years of this sort of work." I am pleased that Mrs. Blake gained so much pleasure by helping with this project.

Alaska archivists Bruce Parham at the National Archives and Records Administration in Anchorage and John Stewart at the State Archives in Juneau uncovered valuable documents dealing with Aline Bradley's medical career and her involvement with the Barnette bank failure. Audrey Parker, formerly of Fairbanks, generously shared information about her grandmother, Genevieve Parker, and hard-to-find photographs of Aline. In addition, I am grateful to Barbara Williams of Hahnemann University, who searched their Archives and Special Collections on Women in Medicine to locate much needed information about Aline's life before coming to Alaska. For Aline's physician's records, I thank Mary Sue Adams, the American Medical Association Researcher at the National Genealogical Society in Arlington, Virginia. Dr. Robert Fortuine of Wasilla, Alaska, enhanced the chapter about Aline with his research about Alaska health issues and his assistance in steering me to other sources of information.

I am particularly grateful to the staff of the Elmer E. Rasmuson Library at the University of Alaska Fairbanks and to Candace Waugaman, who for many years has generously suggested sources and shared items from her personal collection.

For this same interest and assistance, I thank doctors Mary Mangusso, Carol Gold, and William Schneider at the University of Alaska Fairbanks, who helped guide this project. Not only did they act as able advisors, they genuinely shared my excitement with each new discovery during the research process. Additionally, I am indebted to Dr. Beverly Beeton, now retired from the University of Alaska Anchorage, whose shared interest in the social history of Alaska women broadened the scope of this work and whose friendship helped me keep my mission in perspective. Many thanks to Melanie J. Mayer, professor emerita at the University of California, and Sandra Schackel of Boise State University for their attention to detail as they reviewed this manuscript. Their suggestions were invaluable. Elisabeth B. Dabney of the University of Alaska Press deserves special recognition for the vision she had that this project could actually come to fruition. Finally, to all of Alaska's women who have collectively participated in shaping this last frontier, I dedicate this work.

E. T. Barnette's *Lavelle Young* docked on the Chena River, July 23, 1904.
(Rust Family Papers, Subseries 3, Box 2, Folder 216, Archives, University of Alaska Fairbanks)

Introduction

Living in this wonderful land
never could be considered a hindrance to the good life.
With pioneering came material inconveniences,
but it is one's reaction to any difficulty
which may arise that matters—not the problem itself.[1]

A Light in the Wilderness

FAIRBANKS WAS FOUNDED accidentally on the south bank of the Chena River, seven miles upstream from its confluence with the Tanana River, when a sandbar grounded trader E. T. Barnette's steamer in 1901. Destined for Tanacross, farther up the Tanana and near the Canadian border, Barnette had planned to establish a trading post at the halfway point of a proposed railroad between Valdez and Eagle. Stranded, Barnette unloaded his cargo. The next year this enterprising young man met local prospector Felix Pedro, who shared news of a gold strike in the surrounding hills, and a new community was born.[2]

Prior to finding gold in the Tanana Valley, prospectors were busy in the Fortymile, Circle City, and Nome districts in Alaska and in Canada's Klondike. The United States federal government took notice of all this activity and supported Alaska's development by building trails and forts, constructing a telegraph system for the purpose of connecting the military posts, and laying a cable to connect this system with the United States. A federal court was established at Eagle in 1900, and the United States Geological Survey charted the region. Fort Gibbon, on the Yukon River at the mouth of the Tanana, provided some semblance of law and order, and the community of Chena, founded in 1901 where the Chena River flows into the Tanana, was a fur trading center. The United States Army's search for overland routes into interior Alaska gave prospectors additional travel options. The military trail up the Copper River Valley, constructed between 1898 and 1901, had a branch into Fairbanks, and construction of a telegraph system by the army soon produced other paths.[3]

1

Into Barnette's hastily constructed trading post came a rush of seasoned prospectors from played-out goldfields in Canada and other Alaska locations. They rushed to this new area still hopeful that "the sinking of 'one more hole' might compensate for years of back-breaking toil."[4] The following frequently told story illustrates the mind-set of these confirmed fortune hunters:

> At the gates of Heaven a "sourdough" applied for admittance. St. Peter denied his request and stated that there were already too many prospectors within the sacred precincts. The applicant promised that if he were admitted he would rid the place of prospectors. Thereupon St. Peter permitted the "sourdough" to enter.
>
> The newcomer at once sought out his former cronies and soon whispered into the ear of each the "news" of a rich strike in Hell. He mentioned "coarse gold," so many "cents to the pan," "shallow ground," and so forth.
>
> The next morning bright and early each and every prospector slipped away through the pearly gates, purposely left ajar, and stampeded to Hell. Not long after their departure St. Peter intercepted the recent arrival as he, too, was stealing away to follow his fellows. When the astonished saint inquired the reason for his departure, the "sourdough" replied, "You know, there might be something to that report after all."[5]

Miners so poor they had no provisions or capital with which to fund their mining operations streamed into the Tanana Valley, only to meet discouragement when they learned that Barnette accepted only money or furs at his store—no credit was extended. As quickly as they arrived most seekers departed, leaving only thirty residents in the area. Barnette's enterprise was flagging.

Some believed that Barnette began a campaign of exaggerated claims about the amount of gold to entice prospectors and to stimulate business. By January 1903, Abraham Spring, an attorney in Circle who later came to Fairbanks, calculated there were eight hundred people in Chena and Fairbanks, but no mining equipment. Nevertheless, during the coldest winter on record, people poured out of depressed Dawson and headed for the Tanana Valley.

Unlike the earlier stampeders, who came for gold, this second wave of hopefuls was lured by the prospects of business enterprise. These seasoned pioneers had time and experience on their side, and instead of retreating south when the Klondike gold waned, they chose to make permanent homes in the North. Initially lured to Dawson with hopes of quick riches, they moved to Fairbanks content with the slower but more reliable route to the good life—business. When they arrived in February, they were greeted by seven saloons on First Avenue and immediately set out to build several restaurants, a barber shop and newsstand, two clothing stores, a Japanese laundry, a drugstore, and a secondhand store. Commingled with the businesses were lawyers, doctors, and dentists. In March, the Episcopal and Presbyterian churches were established, and in April, Barnette deeded a parcel of his land at the corner of Cushman and Third streets for use as a courthouse and jail

Downtown Fairbanks six months after incorporation, June 1, 1904.
(Courtesy of Candace Waugaman)

site. Eventually, Judge James Wickersham moved the seat of justice from Eagle, over two hundred miles east on the Canadian border, into Fairbanks.

By April 1, 1903, the Fortymile police station had recorded 578 men, women, and children who had passed through en route to the Fairbanks area. Supplies were sparse and prices high, but the pioneers staked town site lots and got down to the business of building a community.[6] Although statistics do not document how many women were part of the early Fairbanks population, it is known that they were present from the beginning.[7] In May 1903, when Ellen Gibson arrived from Dawson with a dream to build and operate a fancy hotel, she claimed to be the sixth woman to call the new town home.[8]

Shortly after Wickersham's arrival Frank Cleary, Barnette's brother-in-law, divided up the community into lots and blocks and charted avenues that paralleled the meandering course of the Chena River. Streets, laid out at right angles to the river, were named for early settlers and government officials, and avenues were designated by numbers, beginning at the waterfront.[9] This geometric pattern is consistent with the development of other frontier towns and, according to historian Richard C. Wade, had deeper meaning. Twentieth-century America was shifting from an agricultural economy to one with industrial roots. This rectangular pattern assigned to city streets gave the illusion of orderliness and represented urban rather than rural living.[10] For the residents of Fairbanks, familiarity with the structure they had previously known Outside may have added emotional comfort. Thus, order and community were introduced on the banks of the Chena.

Most early pioneers acquired lots for their homes through squatter's rights, plus a $2.50 recording fee. On these properties they constructed log cabins made from trees cut on the premises. Although most cabins were small and rustic, they were comfortable and showed the efforts of women's work. Kitchen shelves were lined with jars of their preserved garden harvest, and living and dining rooms displayed cheery flowered wallpaper, lace curtains at windows, carpeted floors, and fine china and silver.[11]

The interior of the Dr. James M. Whitely home.
(James M. Whitely Collection, UAF-1974-0095-00021, Archives, University of Alaska Fairbanks)

In the fall of 1903 the first school opened for thirteen students taught by one teacher paid by city license fees.[12] The Northern Commercial Company, commonly called the N.C. Company, bought Barnette's store, and by autumn five hundred cabins were home to twelve hundred people, who on November 10, 1903, at the direction of Judge Wickersham, held an election and voted to incorporate the town of Fairbanks. A seven-member town council was elected. At its first meeting in December Barnette was appointed mayor, and Judge Wickersham's brother, Edgar, was named deputy United States marshal for the Tanana district. In addition to the top government position, Barnette was appointed alderman and postmaster. At the same meeting the council passed Ordinance No. 1, which allowed for a contract to be made to establish a telephone system.[13]

The third winter after Barnette landed supplies were scarce, but there were rabbits, moose, and caribou to supplement the settlers' diets. However, if people did not have sufficient provisions on hand, they were discouraged from coming, and many who were already there left. Despite this scarcity and the lack of funds that forced the school to close, the people were optimistic they could make something

The interior of the Dr. James M. Whitely home.
(James M. Whitely Collection, UAF-1974-0095-00018, Archives, University of Alaska Fairbanks)

The first public school in Fairbanks opened for thirteen students in the fall of 1903.
(Courtesy of Candace Waugaman)

of Fairbanks. In early November, the Arctic Brotherhood, a fraternal organization started during Klondike days, held a "smoker" that was hailed as "the most important event in the camp" next to the discovery of gold.[14] Later that month the organization christened its new lodge built on Second Avenue by hosting a community-wide Thanksgiving-night ball attended by sixty-seven men and seventeen women. On December 26 the town was incorporated. Fairbanks and her people were stable and established.

As winter progressed, the town council addressed the need for sidewalks, sewers, fire protection, water, electric power and light, garbage collection, and mail service. In May 1904, only two years and nine months after Barnette ran aground, the telegraph and telephone systems were operational, the Episcopal Church opened St. Matthew's Hospital, the smallest coin accepted for trade was a twenty-five-cent piece, the N.C. Company accepted gold dust at sixteen dollars an ounce, and Billie Robertson was the proud owner of the "first and only piano in town."[15] In June, Archie Burns received the contract to build a 305-foot-long drawbridge at the foot of Cushman Street to span the Chena River, and the town council unanimously voted to discontinue the acceptance of gold dust in payment of city accounts.[16] By fall the town boasted three thousand people, who mined $350,000 worth of gold.[17] With fifty-three children enrolled in school, it was necessary to hire an additional teacher and consider construction of a new

The Second Annual Grand Ball of the Tanana Masonic Club of Fairbanks,
February 22, 1906.
(Rust Family Papers, UAF-1963-0054-00044, Archives, University of Alaska Fairbanks)

school building.[18] By the end of the year the amount of gold mined gave the Fairbanks mining region the distinction of being "the third great placer mining district of the North."[19] Fairbanks was no longer a trading post on the banks of the Chena River but a thriving community intent on permanence.

Growth was not without disaster, however. On July 1, 1905, a flood did an estimated $50,000 worth of damage, and a fire on May 22, 1906, destroyed much of the business section, resulting in a $1.5 million loss.[20] After both catastrophes Fairbanksans rebuilt, and the "new town" included a second hospital (St. Joseph's Hospital, operated by the Sisters of St. Ann for the Catholic Church), which opened on Thanksgiving Day 1906.[21] By 1907, the area boasted 5,000 residents, 142 of them enrolled in the public school. A well-supplied business and professional district provided all the merchandise and services required by the residents, and the town fathers proudly boasted that over $3 million had been invested in the construction of the principal buildings. During the summer of 1907, Dr. Aline Baskerville (subsequent marriages changed her name to Bradley then Beegler) and her physician husband arrived in Fairbanks and established a joint medical practice. In addition to providing health care, Aline, a talented, trained singer, helped to organize musical performances that enhanced the quality of life in the young town.

Gold mining dropped off after its 1909 all-time high, and the Fairbanks population declined. However, in 1910 the community was home to 7,675 people, or 12 percent of the territory's population, and was the largest town in Alaska.[22] The

Fairbanks schoolchildren enjoy an outing, November 6, 1905.
(Rust Family Papers, UAF-1980-0034-0001, Archives, University of Alaska Fairbanks)

St. Matthew's Episcopal Church, Reading Room, and Hospital opened in 1904.
(Rust Family Papers, UAF-1963-0054-00058, Archives, University of Alaska Fairbanks)

Downtown Fairbanks was destroyed by fire on May 22, 1906.
(Rust Family Papers, UAF-1963-0054-00051, Archives, University of Alaska Fairbanks)

After the May 1906 fire, the downtown was rebuilt and included St. Joseph's Hospital on the north side of the Chena River. Immaculate Conception Church was relocated closer to the hospital in 1911.
(James M. Whitely Collection, UAF-1974-0095-00121, Archives, University of Alaska Fairbanks)

By 1913, the downtown dock area of Fairbanks was bustling with sternwheelers carrying
supplies and passengers.
(Robert and Jessie Bloom Collection, UAF-1963-0089-00033, Archives, University of Alaska Fairbanks)

federal government continued to pour in money to improve the infrastructure,
even though it was not until World War II that Fairbanks saw any major population growth again.

The expectation that government aid would assist in building Fairbanks was
not unusual. Geographer Isaiah Bowman noted that twentieth-century pioneers
demanded federal assistance to improve their quality of life. "The older pioneer,"
wrote Bowman, "thought in terms of labor rather than of government."[23] More
recent pioneers, he stated, abandon freely their dreams if things do not work out,
seeking the shelter of cities with steady jobs and regular wages. However, for
those who stick to their dreams, "hopefulness is epidemic."[24]

When women's suffrage was debated in Alaska in 1912, Fairbanks women
gathered to address this political issue. Among those who organized a local
campaign was newcomer Jessie Bloom, who had participated in the suffrage
movement in London. At first Fairbanksans did not appear to engage themselves
with the issue, possibly because men generally agreed that women should have
the right to vote. Some, like supporter Bob Bloom, Jessie's husband, who owned
a secondhand store where people regularly gathered to hash over topics of public
concern, believed the female vote would help bolster support from Washington,
D.C., for the development of the territory.[25] Other open-minded men believed
it was the logical thing to do. The bill to enfranchise Alaska's women was the

The Pioneer Women of Alaska organization was founded for women who had arrived in Alaska prior to 1908. Pictured are some of the members participating in a midsummer parade.
(Courtesy of Candace Waugaman)

first law passed by the First Territorial Legislature in March 1913. It was another seven years before ratification of the Nineteenth Amendment to the United States Constitution gave women the right to vote nationwide.

Although Fairbanksans were not overly involved in the suffrage debate, in the summer of 1916 the temperance issue caught people's attention. While on a speaking assignment in Fairbanks on behalf of the Woman's Christian Temperance Union, Margaret Keenan Harrais was offered the job of superintendent of schools, which she accepted. The next year, when the United States entered the First World War and the American Red Cross established a chapter in Fairbanks, Margaret introduced Red Cross programs into the schools to encourage the youth of Fairbanks to support the war effort.

Because World War I siphoned off so many young men, Fairbanks experienced another financial setback. In its continued effort to boost the Alaska economy, the federal government established the Mine Experiment Station, and John Allen Davis moved to Fairbanks during the summer of 1917 to administer this new division. His wife, Mary Lee, was a writer who was enthralled from the beginning with everything she saw and experienced and began to capture it all on paper.

The construction of the federally funded Alaska Railroad, begun in 1917 to connect Seward on the coast to Fairbanks in the Interior, slowed during World War I due to the lack of manpower. Finally in 1923 it was time to celebrate its completion. President Warren G. Harding and Alaska Territorial Governor Scott Bone were on hand in July to drive the "golden spike" at Nenana, fifty miles south of Fairbanks. Excitement was high as hopes for prosperity in Interior Alaska peaked. Although Fairbanks did not immediately see a turnaround in its economy, the trend toward a brighter future was launched. Cheaper and more reliable year-round transportation meant regular access to coal for fuel and to supplies. Large-scale mechanized mining was another benefit that helped pave the way to a stronger economy.

The Women Who Came North

At the turn of the century fewer than 3 percent of Alaska's 45,786 non-Native inhabitants were women, and two-thirds to three-fourths of these were married. More than half of the men living in the territory were single and between the ages of thirty and forty-four.[26] The Pioneer Women of Alaska organization was chartered in February 1916 as a sorority for white women who had come north before January 1, 1908, and had ultimately made Fairbanks their home. One-third of the women who arrived during Fairbanks's first five years were foreign born, with origins mostly in western Europe and Scandinavia. These figures are consistent with those of cities on America's western frontier in the mid-1800s, which benefited from immigrants who brought with them skills and capital.[27] Of the two-thirds of Fairbanks women born in the United States, most were from the Midwest, the plains states, and the West. Twenty-two percent of the American-born members came from California and Washington, whose ports of San Francisco and Seattle supplied Alaska.[28] Most of these women were married and came with their husbands. However, single, widowed, and divorced women also ventured north.

Many early Fairbanks residents came into the Tanana Valley from the played-out goldfields in Dawson. Their 975-mile journey took them down the Yukon River to Fort Gibbon, where they transferred to smaller steamers for the trip up the Tanana River. At the town of Chena they switched to even smaller vessels or walked the seven miles into Fairbanks. Some newcomers came directly from the port cities of San Francisco, Portland, and Seattle to St. Michael on Alaska's western coast. From there they traveled 1,176 miles by steamer on the Yukon River to their new homes. Although expensive and time-consuming, the latter route was luxurious compared to the land trails. Regardless, a few people chose the 365-mile overland route between Valdez in southern Alaska and Fairbanks to make their entrance into the Interior.

Regardless of the time it took or the difficulty of the journey, as soon as women reached their destinations they busied themselves creating homes. References to Fairbanks as "the camp" are found in the early literature. In fact, Fairbanks was

Summer carnivals were a time to gather and purchase supplies for winter. Here, ladies participate in a horseback race on the Fourth of July, 1913.
(Courtesy of Candace Waugaman)

Midnight sun baseball games have always been popular in Fairbanks to take advantage of the twenty-four-hour daylight during the summer. June 21, 1907.
(Courtesy of Candace Waugaman)

founded as a commercial and social center to support prospectors and miners who established camps in the hills around the population center. Those who lived in the outlying camps came into Fairbanks for supplies, and their trips frequently coincided with special community functions such as summer solstice with its midnight baseball game or the two-day Fourth of July celebration.

The first couple of winters in Fairbanks supplies were meager, forcing women to economize and adopt ingenious methods to create comfortable homes. Solid wood banana packing crates were frequently retrieved from the N.C. Company and covered with brightly colored fabric to create end tables. Homemaker and mother Ida Crook recalled that in the winter of 1904 her family ran out of coal oil and candles, and no store carried children's clothing. She recorded, "the only light I had was grease in a saucer in which I placed a wick. I also had to make everything my boys wore right down to their foot wear. I made moccasins and mitts" fashioned from moosehide.[29] Clara Rust, whose descendants continue to live in Fairbanks, recalled that "in spite of our modest surroundings, we were never ashamed of our homes, nor did we apologize for the makeshift arrangements. Rather, we prided ourselves on every new invention to utilize the materials available."[30] By 1915, frame houses became more common, and many were considered luxurious even by Outside standards.

Although cities have a cultural, social, and political focus, above all they are places where people congregate to earn a living. A stable economic base is a prerequisite for these other factors, and women had their hand in the business side of Fairbanks from the beginning. Margaret Brandt, who arrived as a widow, was the town's telephone operator from 1905 until 1938. Single when she came north to Nome, Rae Boas Carter worked at dry goods, fur trading, real estate speculation, money lending, dance instruction, and mining. When she moved to Fairbanks in 1906, she continued her mining interest in the Tanana Valley. With her husband, whom she married in Dawson, Marshia Latimer Lavery came to Fairbanks in 1904 and opened Lavery's House of Quality. Genevieve Boas Parker arrived in Fairbanks as a young single woman and established a candy store, which after her marriage she continued to operate near Anna Shiek's catering business.[31] Cora Madole Meyers hung out her "Madame Renio: Fortunes Told" sign, which she had used in Dawson. When not predicting the future, she earned her living by sewing.[32] Mrs. Godski, widowed in Fairbanks with a small son, found it necessary to take in laundry from the "girls on the Line," a fenced area where local prostitutes worked.[33] In 1907, "five competent lady teachers, including [a] lady principal," educated the community's children,[34] and Dr. Aline Baskerville was available to provide medical treatment.

Influence of Women on Social Organization of Fairbanks

However industrious, Fairbanks women did not spend all of their time homemaking or earning a living. They had public and social lives as well. As in other American frontier communities, women organized themselves into benevolent societies intent on helping the less fortunate and improving the quality of life. The pioneer groups were formed early, men's fraternal organizations such as the Masons and Eagles had women's auxiliaries, and each church had a ladies' guild. The guilds of St. Matthew's Episcopal Church and Immaculate Conception Catholic Church organized annual fund-raising fairs and dances to benefit their hospitals. These well-advertised, multiday events were bazaars at which booths displayed home-baked and hand-sewn items for sale, musical groups entertained, motion picture showings were scheduled at regular intervals, and a Saturday "Charity Ball" drew the town together in a grand finale of music and dancing.[35] In 1907, St. Matthew's proudly reported they netted $1,610.75 from their annual fair.[36] The suffrage debate captured the attention of some Alaska women in 1912, and the next year

Fairbanks women organized themselves into the Women's Civic Club. Monitoring issues related to women and the moral fabric of the community, this club, jointly with the Episcopal Church Women's Guild, operated the George C. Thomas Library until local government assumed that responsibility in July 1942.[37]

When the local American Red Cross chapter was formed in 1917, women were instrumental in its administration and participated in the organization's wartime projects of rolling bandages and knitting socks, sweaters, and afghans. Through the efforts of Margaret Keenan Harrais, superintendent of schools, and Mary Lee Davis, who handled publicity for the Red Cross, Fairbanks women and children raised thousands of dollars in support of the war effort through a special women's edition of the *Fairbanks Daily News-Miner*, school Liberty Bond sales, and Red Cross drives.[38]

In addition to group contributions, individual women provided community service. For example, when the George C. Thomas Library was threatened with closure due to lack of funds in the fall of 1917, Mrs. A. D. Pardee made a financial donation that allowed the doors to remain open. For her generosity the town council publicly offered thanks for her "splendid philanthropy and public-spirited action."[39]

With the right to vote and a heightened awareness of their potential, Fairbanks women wasted no time in getting involved in policy making. Dr. Aline Bradley ran unsuccessfully for a seat on the town council, but this did not stop her from becoming active in other political arenas. As chairperson of the Fourth Division Drys, a Fairbanks women's organization that lobbied for enforcement of prohibition laws, Dr. Bradley established an influential relationship with Territorial Governor John F. A. Strong. Her appointment by Governor Strong to the territory's medical board from the Fourth Judicial Division and her work with him as an advisor on maintenance of the "8-hour law" regulating the workday helped to prepare her for a new career in the law.[40]

Not all women's organizational efforts were directed to benevolent social services. Many with cultural interests were instrumental in bringing the performing arts to Fairbanks. Anna Penketh Caskey, an English immigrant educated at the New England Conservatory of Music in Boston, held the distinction of directing the first opera performed in Fairbanks in December 1906,[41] and Dr. Aline Bradley (then Baskerville) organized the Fairbanks Oratorio Society in 1907 to present religious vocal music. In 1910, Jeanette Drury Clark formed a general choral group that gave performances throughout the winter.[42] The community also had a theatrical group that attracted women who enjoyed performing on stage,[43] and Mary Lee Davis is remembered for her lectures on art and literature.[44]

Some historians believe that one draw to America's western frontier was the lack of a social class structure.[45] However, this theory does not necessarily apply to the North or to Fairbanks. While family lineage and economics were

The living room of a Fairbanks home in 1909.
(Ralph MacKay Collection, UAF-1970-0058-00002, Archives, University of Alaska Fairbanks)

not necessarily considerations for status, a person's length of time in the North afforded a certain prestige announced by membership in the elite pioneer organizations. Geographer Isaiah Bowman stated that in the American West as communities developed, their founding families felt a "sense of proprietorship and accomplishment."[46] This practice applied to early Fairbanks as well and can be seen in the aura of superiority that membership in the Episcopal and Presbyterian churches provided for their parishioners over those of denominations established later.[47] During the early years of development Fairbanks was composed of log cabins of similar size and configuration. Therefore, housing did not delineate status. But it was not long before frame structures replaced rustic dwellings, and these new homes were equipped with accoutrements commensurate with their owners' ability to pay. A woman's dress could also set her apart, and Mary Anderson's Dry Goods and Dress Shop was well known by 1908 to carry "very expensive lines of clothing that the average person could not afford."[48] Of the social class system in Fairbanks, Philip Knowlton wrote in 1916: "There is a refreshing absence of distinction in the honorableness of different kinds of work. Social castes, of course, exist, as they always will while men differ in mental power and moral advancement: but the basis of class distinction is natural and inevitable and not artificial."[49] In death, however, social segregation was requested by some. In 1904, Father Monroe of the Catholic Church was granted the westerly one hundred feet of the community cemetery for burial of his parishioners.[50]

Even though personal adornment, housing, and membership in the "right" church or organization distinguished certain women, the basic social structure of Fairbanks was centered on community-wide involvement in entertainment and service activities. John A. Clark, an early Fairbanks attorney, recorded in his unpublished reminiscences that "'society' consisted of the people who were here [and] those who desired to give parties invited those who were here."[51] He further stated that:

> It was not considered good form to inquire too carefully into the past of your guests, else the list of guests might be unreasonably curtailed. Conversely, if you wanted to go to a party you shouldn't be too particular in investigating the record of your hostess. In fact a good many of the ladies who comprised the society of the town at that time had what was commonly known as a "Dawson past." But then Dawson was on the Canadian side of the line and many cleansing rivers flowed between the two towns, to say nothing of vast virgin forests that covered the land. To a tolerant mind the present and future meant more than the murky past.[52]

Not only did the citizens socialize together, they rallied around anyone in need. Although it was understood that respectable women and children never walked down the "Row" on Fourth Avenue where the prostitutes lived, if one of these women needed assistance due to illness or a burned cabin, other women offered unconditional aid and vice versa. Margaret Murie, who was a child when she came to Fairbanks in 1911, wrote, "There was a good deal of live-and-let-live.... We were all far away from the rest of the world; we had to depend on one another."[53] Sensitivity toward the "sporting women," as prostitutes were called, was not limited to the townswomen. Alonzo L. Maxey, a farmer from the Big Delta area southeast of Fairbanks, traveled to Washington, D.C., at his own expense to testify before the House Committee on Territories in the spring of 1912 to express his belief that certain government officials in Alaska were not conducting business in accordance with the law. One concern of Maxey's was the treatment of the prostitutes, who he believed were "corralled the same as cattle" behind the high board fence that separated their cabins from the rest of town.... It is the Fairbanks Zoological Park," he chastised.[54] In defense of the women, Maxey asserted that "these women are human. There are men of the same class in the town, but they have votes and run at large. These women ... are down, so they are being kicked."[55]

A person's need did not have to be life-threatening to be considered important. In the early days of small one- and two-room cabins most women did not have all of the necessities for entertaining. Borrowing from friends and neighbors was the accepted practice, and, as John Clark remembered, "if a woman had a very nice looking fern it was certain that that plant would be a guest at every wedding or other social affair in the town."[56]

A ladies' summer garden party. Likely the hostess borrowed accoutrements
from her friends in order to entertain such a large group.
(Courtesy of Candace Waugaman)

As in the rest of the country, divorce and separation were increasingly common, but statistics on marital collapse are unavailable for the early days of Fairbanks. However, an article that appeared in the *Fairbanks Daily News-Miner* in
April 1914 hints that the numbers of dissolved marriages may have been high.
On March 30 a rival newspaper, the *Citizen*, published an article questioning the
legality of marriages if a designated waiting period had not occurred between a
divorce and remarriage. After accusing the *Citizen* of criminal action by "questioning as it does the marriage ties that bind Alaskans and the legitimacy of their
children by such marriages," the *News-Miner*'s editor reported that as a result
"every lawyer in town has been consulted by people whom the article worried."[57]
Editor Thompson explained that if the Outside time limit applied to Alaska,
which it did not, "very many people would be affected."[58] Although divorce
apparently did not carry a social stigma, dissolution could create economic hardship for women. Some were forced to rely on their adult children for support or
to resort to menial jobs.[59] However, others, like Margaret Keenan Harrais, who
had a higher level of education or training were able to secure more lucrative
employment and live comfortably.

Signs of Stability

When the railroad connecting the Interior with Seward on the southern coast of
Alaska opened in 1923, Fairbanks hoped for an immediate boost to its population and economy. During World War I military service and railroad construction jobs had siphoned off many of the men, leaving the general area with only

fourteen hundred residents. The outlook was not entirely bleak, however. All along, the federal government had backed the establishment of various institutions that helped Fairbanks survive and ultimately grow. The agricultural and mining experimental stations, opened in 1906 and 1917 respectively, boosted Fairbanks, and the opening of the Alaska Agricultural College and School of Mines in 1922 helped cement the image of permanence. In addition, Fairbanks housed the administrative offices of the United States district courts, the Bureau of Land Management, the Alaska Road Commission, the United States Department of the Interior, the Division of Forestry, and the Alaska Geology Branch of the Agriculture Experiment Station.

Although not an economic mainstay, agriculture interested some residents. By 1920 more than seventeen hundred acres were under cultivation for barley, wheat, and corn, and several dairy farms operated.[60] For Stacia Barnes Rickert, active engagement in farming became her family's financial base. Prior to her marriage, Stacia staked 320 acres of land on the south edge of Fairbanks. She and her husband cleared an additional eighty-five acres and started a farm and greenhouse business.[61] After living in several different Alaska locations Stacia declared Fairbanks home and remarked contentedly in her later years, "I don't see now much chance of living anywhere but dear good old Fairbanks on Rickert's ranch where we have no gold nor silver mines but plenty [of] good things to eat."[62]

Mary Miller, who with her husband ran the Miner's Home hotel and restaurant from 1906 until 1922, shared Stacia's love for the North and commented, "I have no intention of living in the States. Besides the heat down there bothers me."[63] Of course, not all women found happiness in Alaska. After spending most of her adult life in Fairbanks, Catherine McCarthy prepared to move Outside. Her explanation for leaving was expressed curtly when she stated that Alaska "needs younger and stronger women [and besides, I] do not like it and don't know of anyone who does."[64] On the other hand, Mary Kline Bunnell believed Fairbanks had "satisfied the spirit of this pioneer," and many were proud simply to be numbered among the early settlers of Alaska, America's last frontier.[65]

Mining initiated the original settlement of the Fairbanks area, but its growth and development are attributed to its people, whose intangible qualities of loyalty and identification escape measurement. In some cases residents faced deprivation, hardship, and heartache, but as pioneer Agnes Thomas recorded, "it's one's reaction to any difficulty which may arise that matters—not the problem itself."[66] Fairbanks provided a place where women of diverse backgrounds and experiences could join together in a common goal to create comfortable and meaningful lives. Ellen Gibson came from Dawson to begin anew with dreams of business success, Aline Bradley relied on her medical practice for financial support while she embarked on community activism, and Jessie Bloom, an

Irish Jewish newlywed, used the newness of Fairbanks to develop programs for children that became integral parts of life for many families. Margaret Keenan Harrais was a single professional woman when she arrived, and she spent her years in the North working in the field of education and social reform while Mary Lee Davis turned all of her experiences into best-selling books that helped shape the long-range future of Alaska.

From its beginning, women added a sense of grace to Fairbanks. As with other American frontier women, their dedicated hard work and commitment helped shape a solid, multifaceted community that grew quickly into a sophisticated and permanent town.

1

Sarah Ellen Smith Gibson
circa 1860–1908

...there is not another woman
could or would do all I have done
or would of drove a Horse on the road I did
I am positive of it.[1]

Ellen Gibson

THE KLONDIKE STAMPEDE started instantly when the gold-laden *Excelsior* docked in San Francisco Bay on July 14, 1897. News of the "unlikely-looking lot of millionaires" and their glimmering cargo rippled north, and three days later when the *Portland* reached Seattle thousands of curious onlookers crowded to see the treasure brought from the Eldorado and Bonanza creeks in the Yukon Territory.[2] For some time rumors had circulated about a big strike, but no one dared to believe it until proof appeared before their eyes. If Joe and Ellen Gibson did not visit the dock to witness the unloading of suitcases heavy with hundreds of dollars worth of gold, they certainly read the *San Francisco Chronicle* headlines the next day: "SACKS OF GOLD FROM MINES OF THE CLONDYKE [*sic*]."[3] As they did for other Americans weary from the economic depression that began in 1893 and put half the nation's labor force out of work, these tidings revived the Gibsons' broken-down spirits. The situation also provided Ellen the opportunity to develop her business and entrepreneurial skills.

By mid-August thirty-one boats carrying 15,595 hopeful prospectors were headed north to Dawson,[4] a small town tucked away on the Canadian Yukon River that quickly grew into the largest city north of Seattle and west of Winnipeg.[5] At its peak it bulged with thirty thousand residents, and the entire world watched as its inhabitants struggled to realize their dream of riches. Joe Gibson's decision to participate in this unique experience was fueled by lack of employment and a troubled marriage. With bleak prospects for betterment in California, Joe found hope in the lure of the Klondike. Like many Klondikers, Joe and Ellen anticipated that a fresh start in a land of adventure and economic promise would bolster their sagging relationship and fatten their bank account. Aboard the steamer *Elder*, Joe began his journey north in mid-August, leaving Ellen and their two sons, Tom and Elmer, in San Francisco, where Ellen continued to work as a seamstress to earn her living. Joe's departure marked the beginning of a tumultuous phase of Ellen's life as she impulsively stretched her physical and emotional limits in search of an elusive dream.

Joe's letters to his family during his journey to Dawson were typical of his compatriots who chose the arduous Chilkoot (Overland) trail route. He reported a trail "lined with dead horses mules and donkey, 2 meny have gone clean crazy from pur dispair. Men who never did any hard work and never worked in the woods are a pittyful sight to behold."[6] From Lake Lindeman he wrote, "the state of affairs on the trail is past description, all stages of misery from sichness [*sic*] and distress to actual starvation only those with the most money or the strongest will ever get through."[7] Downcast, wet, and cold most of the time, Joe punctuated his description of the conditions with longings for his family and endearments to Ellen: "I send my true love to you dear little wife…good by darling my heart is heavy to-night I am lonesome."[8] An early start, good physical condition from previous employment on the Canadian Pacific Railroad, and determination made it possible for Joe to reach Dawson before winter set in, only to witness many arrivals, discouraged by food and housing shortages, turn back. In his history of the Klondike stampede, Pierre Berton wrote that "those who had been frantic to reach the Klondike were just as frantic to leave it now."[9] It was as though the adventure of getting there was the goal. Apparently Joe had adequate provisions, which quelled any panic he might have felt, and he secured a mining job at 13 Eldorado, fourteen miles outside of Dawson, where he spent the winter in a tent. Although conditions must have been primitive, he ignored Dawson's troubles and remained optimistic. Compared to what was happening in town, his camp life felt comfortable and secure.

In Dawson that winter gold was plentiful, but there was nothing to buy. Men lounged their days away and at night lost thousands at gambling tables while sipping two-hundred-dollar-a-glass whiskey. For one dollar a minute a lonely prospector could "waltz with a girl in a silk dress [and] under certain conditions [he could] buy the girl in the silk dress too."[10] Living in a male-dominated tent city at a mine outside of town made it easier for Joe to economize and stick with his resolve to remain faithful to Ellen. Concentrating on his dream of staking a claim and acquiring a cabin for his family in Dawson kept him optimistic.

In January 1898, Joe wrote to Ellen that she and the boys should plan to join him that summer. His invitation did not include details about his mining profits, but his expectations for the family's financial success were high. Joe predicted that

Ellen and the boys could earn more money than he, and he calculated that within a couple of years the family could save three to four thousand dollars that would allow them to "get a home some place and be some body."[11] If she would bring her sewing machine, thread, needles, and wringer, she could continue her seamstress business and take in laundry. Certainly Ellen was delighted at the economic prospects that Joe described, and she also must have been encouraged at his claim that "I am a changed man I can tell you no strangers for me any more."[12] Undoubtedly Ellen hoped that their seventeen-year marriage was more solidly grounded.[13]

Although the all-water Yukon River route to the Klondike was the longest and most expensive way to reach Dawson, Joe encouraged Ellen to book passage on an Alaska Commercial Company ship, and that summer she and their teenaged sons started north. It is unclear whether Ellen latched on too quickly to some advertised bargain priced tickets or if the steamship company did not fully explain its fare, because she and the boys discovered at St. Michael, on Alaska's western coast, that their tickets took them no further. Penniless but determined to reach Dawson, Ellen refused the company's offer of free passage back to San Francisco in favor of working to earn the money necessary to complete the remaining seventeen hundred miles.[14] When Ellen and the boys finally arrived in Dawson, they found a bustling community of eighteen thousand people that by freeze-up (the onset of winter) had grown to more than thirty thousand. As Joe predicted, the production and care of clothing could be a lucrative business, and Ellen took advantage of her skills when she learned that "industrious washerwomen could make thousands of dollars a year."[15] In September 1898, Ellen staked a gold claim at No. 33 Below Sulphur Creek, and the following February at No. 24 Above Gold Bottom Creek.[16] Later that year she purchased the Montana Steam Laundry from Peter Petersen for five hundred dollars on terms of twenty-five dollars a month.[17] With hired assistants Ellen ran her business for several years while raising her sons, maintaining a prolific correspondence with curious relatives and friends, and managing the family's finances, all of which became more and more her responsibility.

Tom and Elmer Gibson were aged seventeen and fifteen, respectively, when they arrived in Dawson. Like many youngsters in the Klondike, they worked with their father on his mining claim until they became disillusioned by the amount of money and effort that went into the ground only to see nothing come out. Tom moved into Dawson after a year, where he alternately helped his mother with her laundry, worked on the dock loading and unloading freight, and hunted game and fowl to sell to the meat-starved residents. His favorite hunting partner was his younger brother until Elmer grew restless in the transient and unsettled community and moved back to California, where he earned a meager living at odd jobs.[18] In 1901, Elmer wrote to his mother from the Presidio in San Francisco that after getting into "a little trouble" he joined the army using the assumed name "Robert."[19] Insisting that his misfortune was behind him, he asked Ellen to invite

Tom (left) and Elmer Gibson outside their mother's Montana Laundry in Dawson. The young
men supplemented their income by hunting and selling fresh game to the local miners.
(Sarah Ellen Gibson Collection, UAF-1959-0804-00182N, Archives, University of Alaska Fairbanks)

anyone in Dawson who might be traveling to San Francisco to look him up "for
old time sake" even though he sheepishly claimed, "I know I am not much."[20]
Eventually Ellen enticed him to return north, playing heavily on a job offer in her
laundry and Tom's hunting success.

Because of the general economic slump Outside, many women were curious
how the Gibsons fared and what employment opportunities existed. Most of Ellen's
relatives concluded she was getting "rich out in that golden country," but expressed
no interest in joining the stampede,[21] and a Santa Rosa, California, friend who
enjoyed hearing of Ellen's adventures inquired, "Do you have vegetables up there
or do you live on gold dust[?]"[22] Some of Ellen's friends, ready to move north at
great personal sacrifice, desired specific information to help them prepare. Mrs.
G. Rutland, whose husband was terminally ill, wrote that she was desperate to
"work for my babys [*sic*]."[23] Optimistically, she asked for an honest assessment of
conditions in Dawson but boldly declared that even if "I do not here [*sic*] from
you I shall be in Dawson as soon as I can get in, but I will not take my children,"
whom she reluctantly said would spend the time with relatives.[24] Two years later
Mrs. Rutland shared the story with Ellen of her attempt at self-sufficiency. During
the summer of 1899 Mr. Rutland died, the children were sent to a grandmother in

Texas, and Mrs. Rutland sailed north as far as St. Michael. She wrote Ellen several letters from there and sent word of her presence with every Dawson-bound traveler she met. Hearing nothing from Ellen, she assumed the Gibsons had left the Klondike, and Mrs. Rutland returned to California to live on a pension from her deceased husband.[25]

Mrs. William Brunelle had worked previously for Ellen in Dawson but returned to Seattle, leaving her husband to mine. After some time with no word from him she wrote to Ellen asking if she could regain her job in the laundry and if Ellen knew how her husband was getting along. In anticipation of reemployment, Mrs. Brunelle had placed her small son in a Catholic school on the outskirts of Seattle and was ready to return to Dawson.[26]

Ellen's correspondence with another former employee was not as congenial. The laundry accounts showed that she had overpaid an assistant, and Ellen wrote to her asking that the $3.50 error be returned. The stunned woman responded with her own calculations that indicated Ellen actually owed her four dollars.[27] Ellen's indignant rejoinder outlined Mrs. Currie's poor work habits and delinquencies, remarking, "As for me owing you you were not worth what I paid you for the hole [sic] month."[28] Ignoring Mrs. Currie's arithmetic, Ellen concluded her diatribe with the generous remark that "I will make you a present of the extra pay."[29]

Other business matters required more delicate communication. Even though Joe had promised to send Ellen five hundred dollars for her passage to Dawson, she apparently needed more and borrowed from F. S. Osgood, an Oakland, California, friend. In the fall of 1900, Mr. Osgood requested Ellen repay the loan. Explaining his own failed business dealings and personal desperation, Osgood admitted he had not recorded the amount due him, believing Ellen would remember. Almost a year later, debt still unpaid, Osgood made another appeal. Given Ellen's attention to detail, negligence to this responsibility hints that the Gibsons had not enjoyed the economic success they hoped the Klondike would provide. Ellen asked Elmer, then at the Presidio, to visit Mr. Osgood and explain her situation.[30]

In the spring of 1901, Joe received a letter from a Dawson attorney who represented a local physician demanding payment of a long-overdue two-hundred-dollar bill. The letter stated that a few days prior Ellen had seen the firm's law clerk and informed him that they "could not pay and would not until [they] were ready to do so."[31] Although she expected others to understand, Ellen had an unreasonable attitude toward those who desired the same favor, and she requested a legal evaluation before she would give an advance of five hundred dollars to her husband Joe and his two partners. As collateral the men offered their Vulcan Coal Mine. However, the evaluation revealed that they did not have clear title.[32] It is unclear how Ellen handled this matter, but what is obvious is that Ellen paid close attention to business matters that were in her favor.

The disappointment of unfulfilled economic dreams created tension that permeated the Gibsons' relationship, and the loss of their home to fire in the winter of 1903 added stress to an already gloomy relationship. The days of work mixed with cranberry picking, evenings at the theater, and sipping "fine tea" with friends were replaced by the tedium of constant strain and worry.[33] Although she wrote to her friend and former employee Rose Meder, who had returned to Indiana, that all was well, debt mounted, income declined, and Ellen's relationship with Joe eroded. While Ellen continued to run her business, Joe lost interest in expending great effort for minimal return, and he spent more and more of his time and money in local saloons. No longer interested in working the family claim, he took a job as a laborer at the Rock Creek Coal Mine, whose owner, Arthur D. Hiscock, paid Joe's wages directly to Ellen. As Joe retreated to the familiarity of his former ways, Ellen filled the gap his absence created with other companions, one of whom would play a major role in the next phase of her search for happiness and security.

In the summer of 1899, a tent city sprang up at Nome on the Alaska beaches of the Bering Strait, where for thirteen miles rockers and sluice boxes were in motion uncovering a predicted two million dollars in gold. In one week in August eight thousand people left Dawson in search of another rainbow's end. Pierre Berton reminisced, "And so just three years, almost to the day, after Robert Henderson encountered George Carmack here on the swampland at the Klondike's mouth, the great stampede ended as quickly as it had begun."[34] Joe and Ellen hung on, hopeful that something would change the tide, but nothing came close to re-creating those glorious years when Dawson glittered in the spotlight.

Many who remained in Dawson after the dash to Nome considered this the best period. As the town settled back to ordinary business, it gained an atmosphere of permanence. Churches and a library were built, frame houses occupied former cabin and tent sites, and roads were improved. More than one Klondiker remarked the place had finally become "civilized."[35] But Ellen still hoped for riches, and a staid community of nine thousand could not provide the impetus to fuel her dreams. Word in 1902 of Alaska's Tanana Valley gold strike sounded a second chance, and Ellen's new vision began to take shape.

Familiar with Belinda Mulrooney's successful Grand Forks Hotel at the confluence of Eldorado and Bonanza creeks and her Fairview Hotel in Dawson, Ellen envisioned a similar stylish establishment in the new town of Fairbanks under construction on the banks of the Chena River. Because Joe had drained her emotional and financial resources in Dawson, Ellen concluded he had no part in her new venture in another frontier community. However, Hannah Mullen and Will Butler, her choice of business partners and traveling companions, were considered by some to be no better than the man she planned to leave.

Hannah Mullen, Ellen's assistant in the Montana Laundry, had a reputation as a moody woman who insisted on her creature comforts. Her ability to make the rugged spring journey into Fairbanks and adapt to a fledgling mining town came into question. Will Butler, an Irish immigrant, was considered a restless, spendthrift drinker, not to be trusted. Because the most vocal opposition to her choices came from her husband Joe and from William Lane, a jilted admirer, Ellen indignantly disregarded their protests.[36]

In January 1903, Jujiro Wada, the Japanese cook on E. T. Barnette's steamer the *Isabelle*, was sent by Barnette from Fairbanks to Dawson to share the news of a rich gold strike in the Tanana Valley. Hearing this, people poured out of depressed Dawson headed to the new fields, and in February Ellen finalized plans for her venture, which in addition to a hotel included a merchandise store. At the same time Carl M. Johanson, U.S. commissioner at Eagle, went to Fairbanks to assess the mining operations.[37] If Ellen heard his report that the strike claims had been exaggerated, and the same scarcity of provisions and lack of jobs that Dawson had experienced during its stampede were present in the Tanana Valley, she was undaunted, because she proceeded to close down her laundry while Will and Hannah made a quick buying trip to San Francisco.

On April 2 the three executed a legal partnership agreement and prepared to leave Dawson.[38] Driving two horses top-heavy with goods and a dogsled loaded with provisions and Ellen's kitten, the party followed the Yukon River to Forty Mile, which they reached on April 4, then proceeded on to Circle. From there they planned to travel the most direct route into the Tanana Valley, following roughly what is today the Steese Highway. Reports, however, by Judge James Wickersham's party, a few days ahead of Ellen's, warned that a severe blizzard had closed the trail and passage with horses was impossible.[39] Ellen's group had no choice but to continue on the Yukon River to Tanana, wait for the river ice to break up and continue on into Fairbanks by scow.

The month-long trip was arduous. At Tanana, Ellen reported that she and Hannah were "the only white women ever came here there is 50 men and no women here."[40] While harnessing the horse she had driven over the trail, it hit her in the mouth, breaking one of Ellen's front teeth, and her kitten, which had traveled in a box, escaped. It took half a day to retrieve it. Most of the time she was wet and cold, and one of their horses drowned crossing the Tanana River. The week at Tanana provided needed rest and gave Ellen time to reflect on her experience. Recounting the trials she remarked, "I wish I had waited for the boat to run but it is all over now I mean the Hardness of the trip."[41] Optimistically, Ellen turned her thoughts to the future.

In March 1903, Episcopal and Presbyterian church congregations had been established in Fairbanks, and the next month Barnette had deeded a parcel of abandoned land at Cushman Street and Third Avenue for use as a courthouse and jail site, and Judge Wickersham had officially moved his court to Fairbanks. Many people believed that these acts assured the permanence of Fairbanks and

increased its business prospects. Because most of the stampeders were more interested in commercial rather than mining prospects in the new town, this should
have been good news, but regardless of these signs men were streaming out of the
valley shortly after they arrived. Believing that Barnette and Wada had intention-
ally spread lies about the richness of the country caused many residents to dub the
entire event a "fake stampede," and there was talk about hanging Wada. That
Barnette had previously left the territory for Seattle and Wada fled at hearing the
rumor of violence probably averted tragedy.[42]

The initial stampeders were deserting Fairbanks as Ellen arrived on May 25,
1903, but any concern she might have had didn't compare to the joy she felt at being
met by old friends from Dawson who had preceded her. She found a community
of one thousand people, only five of whom were women, and 387 cabins.[43] Some
lots with cabins were selling for as little as ten dollars as disillusioned prospectors
fled the valley. Taking advantage of the cheap land, Ellen, with Will Butler's help,
staked and cleared a 50-by-150-foot commercial lot on First Avenue on which she
planned to build her 30-by-60-foot hotel.[44] Her dream initiated, Ellen staked four
residential lots on which she intended to build rental cabins.[45] In anticipation of
financial backing, she wrote her sons that "the Hotel is mine alone no partners
only Willie he will always be my partner if Hanna stays she will work for wages.
Keep this part to your self only tell [friends] that the business is mine alone so they
need not be afraid to trust me."[46]

Though staples were in short supply, moose, caribou, rabbits, and fowl abounded.
Ellen assessed the situation quickly, and her business sense told her she could make
money selling cigars and liquor by the gallon. "I want whiskey," she wrote to her
son Tom, telling him, "I could get 25 dollars a gallon for it"—twice the cost.[47] In
addition Ellen itemized hundreds of pounds of food and furniture for Tom to ship
to her in preparation for the opening of her hotel, which she predicted would be
finished before the shipment arrived. "But above all," she admonished, "send me
licquors [*sic*] all that is needed in a bar also sigars [*sic*] and tobacco."[48] Liking what
she saw and what she believed the future held, Ellen remarked, "I think I will live
here for some time if I get a start.... I will do well here this next year."[49] Her only
complaint was mosquitoes that swarmed "like a moving mass of bees bussing [*sic*]
around you day and night."[50]

Ellen's new life in Fairbanks included more adjustment than simply starting
her business ventures. Though she was convinced she was better off physically
separated from Joe, to dissolve the emotional bond to her husband required time.
During the first three months after leaving Dawson, Ellen's correspondence to her
sons in the Klondike regularly inquired about Joe. Although Ellen doubted her
husband cared or missed her, she signed all of her letters "Nellie," Joe's pet name
for her, and regardless of the family breakup, Ellen admonished Tom and Elmer
to "be good to [Joe] no matter how he hurt me he is your father."[51] By late June,

Miners heading to the hills around Fairbanks cross the Chena River at Turner Street before 1906. These were the people Ellen hoped would frequent her hotel when they were in town to purchase supplies. *(Courtesy of Candace Waugaman)*

Ellen was settled in her new surroundings, mention of Joe in her letters virtually ceased, and she began to sign them "Ellen." This emotional stability allowed her to focus on raising the money necessary to carry out her business dreams.

When she left Dawson, Ellen hired a friend to manage property she owned, and Tom was in charge of debt collection. Her son was also to find renters for her cabin on the hill and for the former family home in town, which Joe had vacated. To help her get settled and generate immediate cash, Ellen wanted Tom to send her two thousand dollars, the laundry equipment, and a stove she had seen in a Dawson secondhand store, which she could sell in Fairbanks as mining apparatus. She even asked Joe's destitute widowed mother for financial assistance, which frustrated and deeply hurt the elder Mrs. Gibson. Repeated requests for over sixty gallons of various kinds of liquors and a thousand cheap cigars that she could sell for fifty cents apiece topped her list of money-making strategies, and feeling optimistic that it would not be long before she was earning money, she confidently told Tom, "I will repay you before long also I will make more for you."[52]

As predicted, Hannah proved difficult as a business partner. By the time the threesome reached Fairbanks both Ellen and Will Butler were fed up with her

Ellen Gibson on the porch of her Wendall Street cabin in Fairbanks.
(Sarah Ellen Gibson Collection, UAF-1959-0804-00161, Archives, University of Alaska Fairbanks)

temperamental moodiness and wanted to pay off their share of expenses and dissolve the partnership agreement, but Will had no money. Ellen's request to Tom for an additional five hundred dollars for Will's share pushed Tom's civility beyond its limits. Not only did Tom have a low opinion of Will, he had no money, nor did anyone else that summer in Dawson. He hounded Kittie Craig, one debtor, so frequently that he complained, "She runs when ever she sees me, and she don't let me see her often either."[53] In early August Tom despondently told Ellen that he could not send any money or merchandise. "The town is on the hog," he wrote,

> there is people here that have not got a thing to eat. You can't buy yourself a job anywhere.... The groceries you sent for will cost about six hundred dollars and freight about $150.00 and the liccuors [*sic*] about $250.00 and duty besides on some it will make at least a thousand dollars cash. There ain't that much in town.[54]

Tom had less than thirty-five dollars to his name, and he hoped to accumulate over two hundred to see himself through the winter. In addition to his own financial predicament, he found that taking care of himself was a burden:

> By the way I used to here [*sic*] you say that a womans work was never done and this house keeping has made me think so. If I have to keep it up much longer I will be bug house sure. Washing dishes and making bread (I gave that up and would give up washing dishes too only there is no one to do it but me). I have to get a woman to support me decently.[55]

When Ellen heard of the dire situation in Dawson, she insisted that Tom and Elmer join her in Fairbanks. Even though the new community expected shortages

```
                                                           Form No. 2 x.
   GOVERNMENT TELEGRAPH SERVICE,                           25,000-19-6-1902.
          DEPARTMENT OF PUBLIC WORKS,
                  DOMINION OF CANADA.
        The following message was received by the Government for transmission, subject to the terms and conditions printed on the blank form No. 1,
   which terms and conditions have been agreed to by the sender.


   9. FE. SA. H.          13 Paid


                         Chena Alaska 18 Aug. 1903


   Thos. Gibbson,


                  Care Standard Oil Co., Dawson Y. T.


        Come, also Elmer ship freight via N. C. Co.


        payable here bring money.


                         Mrs. Gibbson


   10.56am. 21.
```

This telegram to her son Tom is typical of the demands Ellen made for assistance. *(Sarah Ellen Gibson Collection, Box 1, Folder 90, Archives, University of Alaska Fairbanks)*

that winter of 1903, nothing as desperate as in Dawson was predicted. She told the boys that jobs in wood yards were plentiful, and of course she could use their help in reaching her goals, to which she still clung optimistically. Exasperated, Tom's response was brief and to the point. "But for Christs sake don't forget I dont work in a bank."[56] Ellen, who always needed the last word, had lost patience:

> I can't understand you being broke.... Now Tomy I dont want you to sit down and morn [*sic*] up there but get all your belongings together and come this is a fine country to live in.... Do not let the grass grow under your feet till you are here navigation closes in about 7 weeks.... Come no matter how you get money for your ticket.... I need you so bad there is no work for women here yet—lots for men so all I can say is come I need you don't fail.[57]

As frustration mounted, Elmer, back from the army and fed up with hard times in Dawson, left for Outside, and Joe, unwilling to work hard for minimal return, quit his job and spent most of his time in local saloons. Disappointed by his brother's departure and disgusted with his father's degradation, Tom heeded his mother's wish to join her, arriving in Fairbanks in September in time for a successful hunting season, news of which lured Elmer back north.[58] With income from Ellen's home-laundry business, Tom and Elmer's meat profits, and presumably something from Will's mining efforts, the foursome spent an uneventful winter together.

Downtown Fairbanks, June 25, 1904, a year after Ellen arrived.
(Courtesy of Candace Waugaman)

As soon as the rivers opened in the spring of 1904, Tom returned to Dawson to gather Ellen's remaining personal possessions and make purchases for her that the previous year's finances had prohibited. With money he earned or collected, Tom bought Ellen a hat, hair combs, and some garden seeds, which he shipped to Fairbanks, saying, "I have done the best I could. Hope its all right, there is nothing here so the sooner I get there the better even if I am broke."[59] In July, he started back to Fairbanks, earning some money freighting other people's goods along the way from Dawson to Tanana.

By spring 1905, Ellen's dream hotel was still an illusion, and her Dawson property manager sent devastating news that due to nonpayment of mortgages the bank had foreclosed on her coal property and the two houses.[60] Although Will had staked a twenty-acre placer claim in the Big Delta region of the Fairbanks Mining District in January, he did not have the money to work it.[61] He believed that a temporary move Outside would cure his financial problems, and in August he left for San Francisco to find a job. Immediately, however, he regretted his decision to leave Ellen behind. From St. Michael he wrote, "I am feeling so homesick that I am so sorry that I ever left Fairbanks. I wish I was near you again and you bet your sweet life that I would stay until you were ready to come with me."[62] A day after arriving in Seattle he wrote Ellen that he was already discouraged with business prospects and fed up with the Outside. Unless she promised to join him immediately, he planned to return to Fairbanks. Yielding to Will's tug, in late September Ellen began the five-week journey to California only to learn, when she arrived, that Will had already headed north, apparently unaware that Ellen was en route to join him. Out of money, Will's return trip Outside was delayed. Although Ellen knew that Tom thought little of Will, she directed her son to provide Will with the funds necessary for his return fare.

North side of the Chena River during the spring breakup.
(James M. Whitely Collection, UAF-1974-0095-00036, Archives, University of Alaska Fairbanks)

While waiting for Will to return to California, Ellen learned from a friend that Joe had followed her to San Francisco and was spreading stories of how she had deserted him in Dawson for another man. Angered by his actions, Ellen filed for divorce. Lonely for Will and distraught by Joe's presence, Ellen busied herself with yet another way to make money—real estate ventures. In need of cash for her new business dealings, as before, she wired Tom in Fairbanks to send money. Tom's reply that there was no money to transmit sent shivers down Ellen's spine.

Edward B. Condon, a Fairbanks attorney and Ellen's property manager, refused to turn over rent receipts to Tom, saying he needed the money for his own personal needs. Simultaneously, Ezra Decoto, the Oakland lawyer handling Ellen's divorce, informed her that he could not proceed until she paid him eighty-five dollars—money Ellen did not have.[63] Blaming Condon for her circumstances and in need of some breathing room, Ellen left the city to visit friends in Valley Springs, one hundred miles northeast of San Francisco, while Will worked at a temporary job outfitting dredges on the docks. Discouraged by the tedium, Will wrote to Ellen: "When I go back home to that dear old Alaska I will attend to business closer than I ever did before."[64]

Ellen's disillusionment was compounded by the April 1906 San Francisco earthquake. She returned to the Bay Area in search of Will and her son Elmer, who was also working on the docks. Finding them safe, Ellen learned that Joe was still in town, drunk most of the time, and a letter from Joe's mother put blame squarely on Ellen's shoulders for the failed twenty-one-year marriage. Sharing her outrage with Tom by letter, Ellen instructed him to "write to your grand mother and tell her that your mother is not to blame but it was the raising she gave her lying son."[65]

California had not provided a panacea to Ellen's financial woes, and shortly after she arrived she remarked, "I am getting tired of here already it costs to live here....They want nearly as mutch[*sic*] interest as we pay their [*sic*]....I never want to come to frisco for meny [*sic*] years after I go back for it is the most stingey [*sic*] hole I ever was in."[66] All hope eroded for economic success in California, Ellen returned to Fairbanks during the summer of 1906 to tend to her business, her last hope for independence. As usual, Will had no money for his passage and deferred all travel arrangements to Ellen.

In January 1907, in spite of the fact that her properties were valued at over thirteen thousand dollars, Ellen, usually upbeat and optimistic, lamented that she had "no good news to tell."[67] The Fairbanks Banking Company had sent to San Francisco for her jewelry, pawned there for her and Will's passage back to Alaska, and she filed a lawsuit against Edward Condon for failure to turn over rent money due her. While she was handling these matters, a disgusted San Francisco boardinghouse operator demanded payment of Ellen's bill accrued during her stay. Ellen tried to negotiate a special rate for herself, which elicited an irate response. Not only did the manager feel her charges were fair, she believed she had saved face for Ellen by providing Will with a room alone when all other men had to double up. Indignantly the proprietress asked, "What did I do it for. so as to hide your disgrase [*sic*]. dont think for a moment that I was blind for he was seen coming out of your room in the Mornings. did I not warn you to be carfull [*sic*]."[68] As Ellen attempted to deal with these matters, a persistent health problem was diagnosed as cervical cancer. Unable to treat her advanced symptoms, Fairbanks physician Dr. Sutherland advised surgery in Seattle.

In September 1907, Ellen got her business affairs in order, rented out all of her cabins, and readied to leave. Convinced treatment would be successful, Ellen expected to remain Outside for four to five months, recuperate at Harrison Hot Springs, and return to Fairbanks the following spring. At the time of her departure Will was out at his mine, and as usual Tom assumed responsibility for his mother's welfare. Ellen's biggest concern was that her son pay her debts as money became available, and Tom's was that Will Butler would be a meddlesome bother. From his hunting camp on Fairbanks Creek Tom wrote: "Now you know if any thing is left for Bill to see too I will through [*sic*] up the whole thing. Now this is final with me as you know I don't like him."[69] After arranging for a ten-dollar-per-month allowance for Will, Ellen gave major responsibility to two attorneys before she left on the *Lavelle Young* in mid-September.

In Seattle Ellen underwent surgery, after which instead of resting she worried. She fretted that her divorce was unsettled and fussed because the lawsuit against Condon dragged. And as always, money worries nagged at her. In spite of her

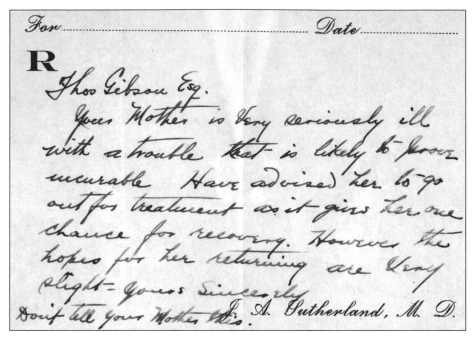

For .... Date ....

R

Thos Gibson Esq.

Your Mother is very seriously ill with a trouble that is likely to prove incurable. Have advised her to go out for treatment as it gives her one chance for recovery. However the hopes for her returning are very slight — Yours Sincerely

Don't tell your Mother this.   J. A. Sutherland, M. D.

In 1907, Ellen's physician, J. Arthur Sutherland, wrote this note to Tom Gibson, explaining his mother's medical condition and prognosis.
(Sarah Ellen Gibson Collection, Box 3, Folder 225, Archives, University of Alaska Fairbanks)

concerns and slow recovery, Ellen filled her hours in bed writing to friends in Fairbanks and enjoying their responses. A letter from Goldie Keeler, the young daughter of one of Ellen's friends, was particularly nostalgic. "I wish you were here," she scrawled in her elementary handwriting, "the house looks lonesome with out you."[70] As if wishing would make it happen, Goldie concluded her letter with the prophesy "I can shut my eyes and see you coming with all the pretty things in the spring."[71] But, as Ellen knew, dreams do not always become reality.

In January 1908, Ellen received a terminal diagnosis. Her sister, Mary Jane Bell of Vancouver, British Columbia, and Tom rushed to her bedside to make her as comfortable as possible. Reduced to skin and bone, Ellen finally admitted she had a "hard fite [sic] for my life and don't know if I will win or not."[72] Will, unable to get together the money to make a trip to Seattle, attempted to comfort Ellen through the mail with the assurance that if she did not recover she need not worry, "for I will do anything to please you and I promise you that although your sons and I can't get along together that for your sake alone I will not start any trouble."[73] With a photograph of her favorite dog, Dandy, on the bedside table, and her son and her sister by her side, Ellen Gibson, in her late forties, died on Saturday, May 17, 1908.[74] She was buried in a Seattle cemetery. As he had promised, Will Butler was amicable and deeded most of the partnership holdings to Tom and Elmer.[75]

By the time Ellen left Fairbanks in the fall of 1907, downtown had developed into a sophisticated shopping district. This photograph was taken just weeks before Ellen left for Seattle.
(Robert and Jessie Bloom Collection, UAF-1972-0108-00002N,
Archives, University of Alaska Fairbanks)

Still unable to settle down, Elmer moved Outside shortly after his mother's death. In California he learned the blacksmith trade, then moved to Nevada to put his skills to use. In 1909, while riding a horse at a fair in Elko, he was thrown and trampled. Serious injuries required several surgeries, but Elmer never regained his strength. Word filtered back to Tom in Fairbanks in 1911 that Elmer had died.[76]

Will Butler continued to live in the Fairbanks area until 1909, when he moved his mining operation to Little Creek near Ophir City in southwest Alaska.[77] He eventually married and lived in Fort Yukon, where he served as deputy marshal.[78] It is unclear whether or not Ellen and Joe were ever granted a divorce. Joe was last known to live in San Francisco.

On January 14, 1910, Tom married Fairbanksan Anna Mae Eisenberg, to whom he was devoted for over fifty years. He supported his family in various business enterprises related to his meat market, automobile repair, and boat building.

When Ellen Gibson came north in 1898, her only assets were a sewing machine, laundry equipment, borrowed money, and a passion to become a financial success. She was a relentless believer that her business schemes would work, but she was always short of money. Escape from disappointment and emotionally draining personal relationships became a pattern that offered the promise of a more inspired life and a refuge from the past. By the time Ellen left Fairbanks permanently in the fall of 1907, the town had grown to five thousand residents who enjoyed a stable infrastructure. Even though Ellen never realized personal success during her four years living there, she had participated in the initial settlement of the mining camp and should have felt some personal pride in this accomplishment. Unmistakable tension permeated Ellen's fiercely independent life, but the power of love and hope made her believe in her men and strive for a dream. Physical illness deflated her spirit, but only death ended her restless search for an elusive dream that she always believed could become reality.

Ellen had this photo of her dog, Dandy, at her hospital bedside in Seattle.
(Sarah Ellen Gibson Collection, UAF-1959-0804-00137, Archives, University of Alaska Fairbanks)

2

Aline Chenot Baskerville Bradley Beegler
1867–1943

*Barnette was the leader of the claim-jumping,
miner-robbing gang which held this camp by the throat
since its inception. With Barnette Courts and
Barnette Juries, the people had no redress....
Now comes the most wonderfully terrible
part of this tale.[1]*

Aline B. Bradley M.D.

FRENCH-BORN ALINE CHENOT trained as a singer in Paris, a doctor in Philadelphia, and a lawyer in Fairbanks. Juggling this unlikely combination of
careers, she found her niche in the North, where she flourished amidst sorrow and
trials, joy and opportunity. Born in Paris on December 18, 1867, to Jacques and
Louise Renaud Chenot, Aline lived in Europe until 1886, when at age nineteen she
immigrated with her family to the United States. Her older sister, Louise, eventually married German-born Benedict Stalen and lived in Elgin, Illinois, where he
worked at the watch factory by that name. Her younger sister, Anna Adele, earned
degrees from the University of Chicago and Smith College and had a career as a
professor of French at Western College for Women in Oxford, Ohio, and Smith
College, from which she retired in 1944 after thirty-three years of service. A
brother, Emil, settled in Los Angeles.[2]

On April 5, 1894, Aline married Thomas Hardy Baskerville of New York. Ten
years her senior, Hardy, as he was called, was a practicing physician in Pennsylvania. Possibly inspired by his work, Aline abandoned her lifelong plan to be a
professional singer in exchange for a medical career. However, in the 1800s, the
idea that women should be trained as physicians was met with animosity. In fact,
as late as 1872 the German anatomist Theodor von Bischoff preached that because
of woman's smaller brain, her physical weakness, and her gentle nature she was
unfit for medical science. He argued further that "by both the divine and natural

order, women lacked the rare ability to work in the natural sciences and especially medicine."[3] Nevertheless, closed doors to women at the existing American medical schools resulted in the opening of women's medical colleges in Philadelphia, New York City, Chicago, and Baltimore. Begun in 1850, the Woman's Medical College of Pennsylvania was considered the best of the four because of its early beginning, capable leadership, and unusual local support. By the turn of the century, when Aline was ready to begin her training, coed opportunities at American universities were emerging, and the women's medical schools began to close for lack of funds and students. However, the University of Pennsylvania Medical School continued to bar women from admission until World War I. Therefore, Aline's choices were limited if she planned to attend school in Pennsylvania, where she and Hardy lived.

She graduated from the Woman's Medical College of Pennsylvania in 1903.[4] Following her internship the doctors Baskerville left their apartment on Lombard Street in Philadelphia and made a new home in Economy, northwest of Pittsburgh, where Aline was licensed to practice in Beaver and Allegheny counties. There Aline provided examinations for the Lady Maccabees, the women's branch of the men's fraternal insurance group called Knights of the Maccabees.[5]

In 1907, when Aline was thirty-nine years old, Hardy's chronic asthma forced the couple to seek the cooler, dryer air in Alaska. Arriving in Fairbanks during the summer, they found a bustling community of five thousand people, and Aline indulged her trained soprano voice and immersed herself in the seasonal performing arts scene. Days before her first concert, on August 11, her talent was praised when the *Fairbanks Daily Times* proclaimed, "Dr. Aline Baskerville Will Make Her First Appearance and Her Reputation Has Already Preceded Her."[6] Reporters said she was "one of the best singers" who had ever come north, and after performing "Just a Song at Twilight" she was dubbed "a most valuable acquisition to the music circles of Fairbanks."[7] A week later she performed a duet and a solo at the Presbyterian Church services at which Reverend S. Hall Young, the pioneer missionary who founded the Presbyterian Church in Fairbanks in 1905, preached.[8]

After making a name for herself musically, Aline opened a medical practice and became the second woman to practice medicine in Fairbanks—Dr. Dora Fugard preceded her in 1903.[9] Apparently Aline and Hardy felt comfortable in Fairbanks because by fall they were ready to experience their first Alaska winter ensconced in what a friend described as a "picturesque large log cabin" that they bought at the corner of Eighth Avenue and Cushman Street.[10] However, within a year this contentment turned to profound sorrow.

On September 8, 1908, Thomas Hardy Baskerville died in St. Matthew's Hospital, from an inoperable spinal tumor. Two days later more than one hundred Fairbanksans paid their respects at a funeral service conducted by Reverend Betticher at the Episcopal Church. This was quite a tribute to a man who had lived in the community only a year, but it illustrates the tight bonds formed quickly on

Aline played a leading role in the operetta "Erminie" in 1909. Left to right: Tommy Carpenter, Martha Hickman, Edith Ryan, Aline Bradley, Mrs. Frank Hespick, Lila Barter, Mrs. McKeaon. *(Rust Family Papers, UAF-1963-0054-00069, Archives, University of Alaska Fairbanks)*

the frontier, where reliance on each other was not just part of the social fabric but an integral part of survival.

The newspaper article announcing Hardy Baskerville's death described Aline as "almost prostrated over his death."[11] Therefore, it must have caught the community by surprise when three and a half months later, on December 21, Aline married James Freeman Bradley, a tall, handsome Canadian miner. The couple had met earlier that year when James guided a hunt for Aline and Hardy. The story has it that, shortly after Hardy's death, James approached Aline, saying he had fallen in love with her on that trip and wanted to marry her. After the wedding James moved into Aline's log cabin house on Cushman, where she simply changed her name on the sign that advertised her medical practice. Although their union was hasty, a family friend described their relationship as very happy.[12]

Aline affiliated with the Presbyterian Church, where she was choir director and a member of its Ladies' Aid Society, which was organized about the time she arrived in Fairbanks. In 1909, the women compiled a cookbook of members' favorite recipes to which both Bradleys contributed. Aline provided practical instructions to puree potatoes, peas, and beans. The introduction to a reprint edition of this cookbook suggests that in consideration of her profession as a doctor these may have been designed as baby food or nourishment for the sick, while her recipes for a simple French ragout and lettuce salad with French dressing suggest her heritage and a need for efficiency. The final section of the cookbook contained

Aline on the porch of her office. She used the same office for the entire twenty-three years she practiced in Fairbanks, changing her name sign with subsequent marriages.
(Robert and Jessie Bloom Papers, UAF-1963-0089-00227, Archives, University of Alaska Fairbanks)

recipes submitted by men, and J. F. Bradley's instructions for cooking moose began with the tongue-in-cheek advisement to "first catch your moose."[13]

Beginning with her first days in Fairbanks Aline delighted in sharing her musical talent with the community. In November 1910, she was part of a quartet that presented Van Alstine's "Love Light" at the musical portion of the annual St. Matthew's Hospital fund-raising event.[14] On a regular basis Aline performed with the Fairbanks Choral Club, and one year she served as director of the Fairbanks Oratorio Society. Aline so generously shared her talent that omission of her name in reporting a particular concert caused the *Alaska Citizen* to chide the *Fairbanks Times*, its competing newspaper. Charging the *Times* with "cheap journalism," the *Citizen* warned that if Aline, a prominent Fairbanksan, endured repeated slights, she may become "discouraged from giving her services free for the entertainment

The Ladies' Aid Society of the Presbyterian Church. Aline and her husband, James Bradley, contributed to the organization's cookbook in 1909.
(James M. Whitely Collection, UAF-1974-0095-00058, Archives, University of Alaska Fairbanks)

of the public."[15] However, changing events in Fairbanks had more to do with out-lining a new path for Aline's interests and career than did bruised feelings.

Little was known about E. T. Barnette when he founded Fairbanks in 1903. However, by 1911 every resident had an opinion of him. In his biography of Barnette, Alaska historian Terrence Cole recounted "that Captain Barnette had both more money and more enemies than any man in Alaska."[16] But, according to Cole, Barnette had no idea how deeply hated he was by these enemies until the consolidated Fairbanks Banking Company/Washington-Alaska Bank unexpectedly closed its doors in January 1911.[17]

Caught unawares by the closure, the community charged Barnette and the bank's directors with mismanagement and fraud. Angry depositors formed a representative committee of seven—six men and Aline—to investigate.[18] When Barnette, who had been Outside at the time the bank collapsed, finally returned to Fairbanks in mid-February, the community felt relieved that an explanation would be forthcoming and justice would be done. Imagine their disbelief when Barnette had no acceptable solution to the problem and a grand jury didn't find enough wrongdoing to indict him.[19] An editorial in the *Fairbanks Weekly Times* warned that "wildcat banks" could lawfully operate in the territory, and "in the absence of laws necessary to protect unsuspecting depositors from financial trick-sters, it is plainly up to the people to look out for themselves as best they can."[20] The same newspaper reported that E. T. Barnette and his wife, Isabelle, had slipped out of town the previous night in a "double-ender" drawn by a white horse. Disgusted with the corruption, the secrecy of this affair, and the way the case was handled,

Aline and four other Fairbanks women formed a new depositors' committee to take action.[21] Two hundred twenty-five depositors attended the first meeting that Aline called on a Tuesday evening in early April, at which a police escort protected her from threats made by a known community troublemaker. Convincingly, she shared the results of her research into the case, and the depositors voted without dissent

> to further the prosecution of Captain Barnette on the charge of embezzlement; to ask the court to call a special grand jury; to ask the court to remove Receiver Hawkins; to ask for the appointment of the special accountant, and lastly, the depositors present voted to pledge themselves to the extent of five per cent of their deposits to assist in the investigation of the bank situation and the employment of the best legal advice obtainable.[22]

The day after the meeting Aline and her committee were praised by the local newspapers for the "spunk" they demonstrated in trying to get to the bottom of the situation. As a result of this initiative, both the *Fairbanks Weekly Times* and the *Fairbanks Daily News-Miner* pledged to do more aggressive investigative reporting. Working in concert the editors believed they could sleuth out the truth. To maintain momentum Aline shared her opinions with Territorial Governor Walter Clark, who highlighted the following passage in her letter to him:

> That Grand Jury was a wonderful body of men—a few may have been good men—four were in debt to the bank; two were men of notorious character; one of them lives at a nominal rent in Barnette's house, and shamelessly saw Barnette's attorney every day. Barnette's subsequent actions showed that he knew everything that transpired in that Jury room. He had come here to quiet a few dangerous large depositors, and see that that grand jury did not harm him—which it did not. THE FAILURE TO INDICT WAS NO SURPRISE TO THE PUBLIC.[23]

A petition outlining the details of the case and Aline's analysis of the jury was presented to the District Court for the Fourth Division of Alaska and to Governor Clark. But the "most wonderfully terrible part of this tale," she explained, was that F. W. Hawkins, one of the bank's cashiers in on Barnette's scheme, was appointed receiver during the litigation for a salary of four hundred dollars a month.[24] Aline pointed out that Hawkins was still in this position despite cries from depositors. The women's committee urged the following:

- That Judge Overfield be replaced by Judge Thomas Lyons of Juneau.

- That Francis J. Heney, an expert banking accountant (in their opinion) and prosecutor be appointed at the depositors' expense to review the books and work with the district attorney and the committee's attorney, Bion A. Dodge, to bring the guilty to justice.

- That two or more security guards be appointed to watch over the jury-selection process.

- That Hawkins be replaced as the bank's receiver.

The dramatic conclusion to her appeal urged clandestine secrecy:

> Do not ask for assistance from Delegate Wickersham, for we do not know on which side he would stand, and we can afford to take no chances. The manner in which you will help us, we leave to your goodness and discretion. We are moving as quietly as possible, so as not to let the other side know what we are doing.[25]

While Aline urged Governor Clark to move secretly and quickly on this matter, W. F. Thompson, the *Fairbanks Daily News-Miner* editor, who had pledged to investigate this case, moved faster. On April 10, Thompson wrote to Delegate James Wickersham in Washington, D.C., to ask for much the same things outlined by Aline's women's committee. A month later, Wickersham replied by telegram that he would send an investigative agent as soon as practical. Thompson's response was revealing:

> The people of Tanana will be grateful for your action. Please remember that past investigations made in Alaska by department officials have been boys' play and jokes, and assure yourself personally that only high-class men are sent to conduct this investigation.[26]

Surprisingly, a mid-June Fairbanks newspaper article warned that E. T. Barnette was en route to the Tanana Valley aboard the first through sternwheeler of the year. Once there, a *Fairbanks Weekly Times* reporter asked Barnette, "Why did you come back?" Barnette responded, "Why shouldn't I come back?"[27] The conversation stalemated. Purportedly Barnette was still trying to work out the bank's problems and repay depositors their accounts.

The investigation that ensued led to the ultimate arrest of Barnette in late 1911, but a year later his eight flamboyant attorneys waged a good battle on his behalf. Out of eleven indictments against him on such charges as making false reports, perjury, and embezzlement, only one misdemeanor charge was proved. Despite the prosecution's request for imprisonment, Judge Thomas Lyons fined Barnette only one thousand dollars.[28] Based on his accumulated wealth, this was hardly punishment. Hundreds of ruined Fairbanksans believed it was their money that Barnette used to buy his freedom in what W. F. Thompson called the "rottenest judicial farce the North has ever witnessed."[29] Frustrated by the turn of events, Aline retaliated.

On January 12, 1913, Aline and her committee staged a dramatic conflagration on the frozen Chena River at the foot of Cushman Street, where they burned three effigies representing John L. McGinn and John A. Clark, two of the bank's attorneys, and one labeled "Justice." Hundreds of townspeople turned out to cheer the women's vengeful effort to even the score with Barnette and his men.[30] However, according to her friend Jessie Bloom, for her actions Aline was snubbed by some Fairbanksans all the years she remained in the territory.[31] In spite of this, Aline's perseverance paid off when, three months later, the first legislature to convene in Alaska enacted the Territorial Banking Act. Except for national banks, all Alaska banks were now under territorial government regulation for the first time.[32] Aline's efforts were rewarded and her influence was felt Alaska-wide.

With the bank failure case behind her Aline concentrated on her medical practice and redirected the focus of her life. The Fairbanks City Council elected Aline City Physician from a slate of four applicants at an October 1913 meeting.[33] In this public health role, Aline made a report to the council outlining ventilation deficiencies in the school building, which received immediate attention. Additional concerns included medical care for indigents and dairy inspection to ensure the safety of milk. The latter resulted in passage of legislation for quality control. Aline filled this position herself, for which she received fifty dollars a month (later seventy dollars), for a year and a half until April 1915, when the city council abolished the office. During her tenure as city physician, Aline was appointed by Governor J. F. A. Strong to the Territorial Board of Medical Examiners.[34] Possibly at his urging Aline began self-directed study of the law and intended to take the Alaska bar exam. Undoubtedly these medical appointments enhanced Aline's image and exposure in the territory, which enabled greater recognition in the political arena on important issues about to become public. At the same time Judge James Wickersham noted in his diary that he had a "long talk about political conditions with shrewd Mrs. Dr. Bradley."[35]

Like many Alaskans, Aline was caught up in the volatile prohibition debate. An active member of the Woman's Christian Temperance Union (WCTU), she also chaired the Fourth Division Drys, the women's group formed to push for the Bone Dry Law after the wild and drunken 1914 railroad bill celebration (see Chapter 3). Along with Margaret Keenan Harrais, Aline, who also served as Legislative Superintendent for the group, was credited with swaying the vote in the Fourth Division on election day 1916, when Alaskans decided two-to-one in favor of prohibition (see Chapter 4).[36] In addition, Aline worked with Judge Wickersham, Alaska's delegate to Congress, to secure territorial control of school funding. When Congress passed the Bone Dry Law in February 1917, Aline was one of three individuals, and the first in Fairbanks, to whom Wickersham telegraphed the news.[37] By spring 1918, Governor Strong was pleased to report that arrests and crime associated with alcohol had decreased dramatically in the first two months of that year, and C. L. Vawter, United States deputy marshal at Tanana, predicted that when the last drop of cached alcohol disappeared, "all Alaska jails will go out of business."[38] Now that laws were in place to control the manufacture, importation, and consumption of alcohol, Aline's interest turned yet again to other matters.

A reimbursement check from the Women's Civic Club made out to Dr. Aline Bradley, March 13, 1917. This women's group monitored issues related to women and the moral fabric of the community. In addition, they helped operate the community library.
(Courtesy of Candace Waugaman)

Although Aline accepted reappointment to the Territorial Board of Medical Examiners in September 1917, her study of the law under Fairbanks attorney Albert R. Heilig was sufficiently complete for her to take the bar examination.[39] On October 2, 1917, the *Fairbanks Daily News-Miner* announced that Aline passed her oral and written tests, and the three-member examining committee—which included attorney John A. Clark, whom Aline hanged in effigy several years earlier—recommended she be admitted to the Alaska bar. However, her husband's lack of American citizenship stalled the process.[40] At the same time Aline made an unsuccessful bid for a seat on the city council running on the Independent ticket. In fact, of six candidates, Aline had the fewest votes.[41] Being a relative newcomer to Fairbanks may have had something to do with her dismal defeat. The newspaper article that announced the results noted that most of that election's winners were pioneers "having been in the North since the early days of the Dawson stampede."[42] Aline's mere nine years in Alaska may have been a hindrance to her success.

James Freeman Bradley was born in Nova Scotia, Canada, and as a teenager he moved to Missouri with his adoptive parents. Under the impression that his adoptive father had taken care of the citizenship matter long ago, James thought he was an American citizen and in fact had voted in several Fairbanks elections.[43] Nevertheless, his citizenship could not be proven, and it was necessary for him to have a naturalization hearing, which was challenged on a legal technicality.[44] Before the question could be settled, James died at home of pleuropneumonia at age fifty-nine on November 29, 1918.[45] This then raised the question of Aline's citizenship, since her marriage to a Canadian made her a subject of Great Britain. Because her first marriage made her an American, and she planned to remain in Fairbanks, Aline argued for her American citizenship.[46] However, it was not until October 1919, when she married her third husband, Michael Beegler, himself a naturalized American, that her citizenship question was resolved. She was finally

Aline on the porch of her office shortly after she married her third husband, Michael Beegler.
(Courtesy of Audrey Parker)

admitted to the Alaska Bar in November 1920, more than three years after passing her exams.[47] On March 5, 1921, Aline became the first female attorney to appear before the Fairbanks bar.[48]

As before, Aline's period of widowhood was measured in months. According to one source, only weeks after James Bradley's death the first marriage proposal arrived and they continued until eleven months later on October 22, when Aline married Michael Beegler, a miner of German descent who came north in the 1898 stampede.[49] Immediately after the marriage, performed by Presbyterian Church minister Wallace Sutton Marple in Aline's Cushman Street home, the newlyweds left to spend the winter Outside visiting family and friends.[50] A miner from Livengood, Michael had established the practice of spending the harsher half of the year in a warmer climate, and apparently Aline accepted this custom, as they spent the next ten years this way. Because summers were spent in the Livengood Mining District, Aline's practice of the law was limited, but in the fall of 1922, the city council selected her as city magistrate and legal adviser for a salary of fifty dollars a month.[51]

By 1923 Aline was fifty-six years old, and evidence of her medical and legal practices declined. But that does not imply that Aline shrank from view. In fact, quite the contrary. In July, Aline made history as aviator Carl Ben Eielson's passenger on the first flight to Brooks (Livengood). The compass-directed trip took only fifty-five minutes at an altitude of four thousand feet and cost Aline eighty-five dollars. Thereafter, both Beeglers preferred air travel over the weeklong river trip they had

Aline and Michael Beegler (far right) on board the *Aleutian* sailing Outside. The Beeglers moved out of Alaska the summer of 1930 and relocated to Southern California.
(Courtesy of Audrey Parker)

known.[52] At one point Michael remarked that the only way to beat expensive river travel into the Livengood Mining District was roads, but after the Farthest North Airplane Company began its service, flying became his preference.[53]

In 1929, the Beeglers bought a house in Southern California, where they had spent the past few winters. When they returned to Fairbanks in the spring of 1930, it was only to settle business affairs and prepare to retire Outside. A difficult task for Aline was the sale of her beloved log home on Cushman Street. The newspaper advertisement announcing its availability described beautiful furnishings, three bedrooms, hardwood floors, hot water heating, and lots of closets. Of course, its central location was played up as a selling point. By early summer Michael had sold most of his Livengood mining interests, and the Beeglers prepared to start south. On July 10, 1930, Michael and Aline left Fairbanks for the last time, headed to Seward, where they boarded the steamer *Aleutian* for their passage Outside.

In June 1931, Michael and Aline attended college commencement exercises in California for Franklin Zimmerman, son of Aline's good Fairbanks friend Mary Zimmerman. The day after, Michael suffered a paralytic stroke and lost the use of his arms and legs. Five weeks later, on July 17, he died in Highland Park, a Los Angeles suburb, at age seventy-three. Ed Wickersham, brother of Judge James Wickersham, served along with other former Alaskans as pallbearers at the funeral.[54]

Aline continued to live in the Los Angeles area for another twelve years and managed some Fairbanks-area mining interests from afar. She died of heart failure in Pasadena on June 19, 1943, at the age of seventy-five. Although she had lived Outside for more than a dozen years, her Alaska roots remained strong, and her Fairbanks friends Bob Bloom and Mary Zimmerman handled her estate.

Aline showed tenacious courage as she moved through adulthood in her roles of physician, lawyer, political activist, and always wife. Her cunningness provoked some and impressed others, but no matter how she affected people her energy, excitement, and intelligence allowed her to reach new heights. Although only an ethereal image of Aline remains in the North, she had a hand in shaping Alaska's public health policy and its banking laws. She was the second female physician in Fairbanks and the first female lawyer. She played a leading role in early Fairbanks cultural enhancement and in local and state legislation. Aline's commanding presence caused family friend Meta Bloom Buttnick to remark, "Daddy admired her. Mother obeyed her. We all loved her."[55] Those watchwords could serve as Aline's epitaph.

Tag for a Christmas gift from Aline and Michael Beegler to
family friend Franklin Zimmerman.
(Courtesy of Candace Waugaman)

3

Jessie Spiro Bloom
1887–1980

*There was a sense of quiet and peace
in the Interior of Alaska around Fairbanks in those days,
we truly were isolated, and were dependent on each other
and on our own inward resources for our
entertainment and spiritual comfort.[1]*

Jessie Spiro Bloom

E ARLY ON A JULY MORNING in 1912, Jessie Bloom first saw Fairbanks from the deck of a sternwheeler on the Chena River. The boat's "whistle blew, the dogs took up the cry, and we were at the dock," Jessie later recorded.[2] After introductions to the townspeople who customarily gathered to greet the steamers, Bob, Jessie's husband of two months, led her to his general store a block away, which she described as a jumble of guns and trapper's supplies. An hour later, the Blooms walked to the Tanana Bakery on Second Avenue for breakfast. Mrs. Driscoll, the proprietress, brewed Jessie "a special pot of tea ... while Bob took his coffee."[3] Years later Jessie believed that maintaining their independence in such ways contributed to the success of their sixty-two-year marriage. Thus began Jessie's life in Alaska, a life of hope for a frontier community; a life of tradition—and always, the dream for a permanent home.

Of Lithuanian Jewish stock, Bob and Jessie were both raised by parents who had immigrated to Dublin, Ireland, in the early 1880s. When Nicholas I ascended to the throne of Russia in 1825, Jews lived in autonomous communities governing themselves by their own civil, criminal, and ritual laws. Thirty years later Russian politics intruded into Jewish society and changed the foundations of Russian-Jewish life.[4] Oppressive tsarist legislation and severe conscription policy intensified the government's movement to assimilate all Jews into mainstream Russian culture. Many were forced out of positions they had already achieved, which halted their progress and resulted in diminished economic prospects. Jews realized that if they intended to maintain their identity, they must do so outside of Russia.[5] Bob's and Jessie's parents were among the 2.5 million eastern European Jewish immigrants who settled in western Europe beginning in 1880 in search of religious freedom and economic opportunity.

Born in Shavli, Kovno, Lithuania, on October 15, 1878, Bob was a young boy when he came to Dublin, and even in later years Jessie said he was "almost as Irish as 'Paddy's pig.'"[6] In 1897, Bob immigrated to Seattle, where he worked and lived with his Uncle Semach.[7] A year later he "got bitten with the gold bug" and walked over the Chilkoot Pass into Dawson, where he halfheartedly mined until 1904, when he joined the rush to Interior Alaska.[8] In Fairbanks he alternately prospected and peddled until he admitted that the latter was more lucrative, and he opened a general store. Although Bob did not expect his business or the community to endure beyond the life of a placer mining camp, Fairbanks fooled him, because by 1912 there were stampedes to other camps and Fairbanks became the supply center. Later Jessie proudly recalled that "he built up a reputation for honesty and integrity that was part of the growth of Fairbanks, always feeling that the camp's potential was limitless—he was a dreamer."[9] He emerged a successful business-man and a dedicated community leader.

Jessie Spiro was born on December 21, 1887, in Dublin, where she grew up with a sister and two brothers in a comfortable middle-class home on the banks of the Grand Canal. Her childhood days were spent watching horse-drawn barges car-rying loads of turf on the canal and enjoying the pageantry of the red-coated gar-rison sentries from a nearby army barracks marching in their Sunday-afternoon parades. Visits to museums, art galleries, and the botanical and zoological gardens were frequent weekend outings. Jessie's mother had great respect for books and initiated a family tradition that allowed each child a card at the public library when he or she turned twelve years old. Mrs. Spiro supervised the ceremonial acquisition of the card and the choice of reading material until the child had read a specific list of British classics. Once achieved, the children were free to select their own read-ing materials. Access to these cultural and educational institutions was considered a blessing.[10]

Jessie's mother helped found the Dublin Hebrew Ladies' Charitable Society, an organization designed to aid the large number of less fortunate Jewish immigrants who were taking refuge in Dublin. The children of members were expected to help by running errands and delivering messages, and in this way, Jessie said, "we learned to take our part in the community in the easy way, just drifting into it, because it was the thing to do."[11]

Jessie's formal education began at the predominantly Protestant St. Peter's School. This was a "period of rather strict discipline, which I feel may have influ-enced my outlook in later years, because we did have some self-discipline as we grew older."[12] Her fourth-grade teacher was "an old maid [who] seemed to be very frustrated, and took her ire out on her pupils. I seemed to come in for a particular share of her wrath."[13] However, Jessie speculated that

> the freedom we had in the home, made it difficult for us to fall in line with the stricter attitude in school. At home we were permitted to take part in any conversation that took place at the table, and in other ways were treated as personalities. There was no lack of discipline in the home, but both Mother and Father appreciated our individualities. We did not have that atmosphere so common at that time, that children should be seen and not heard.[14]

When Jessie was ten years old she was diagnosed with St. Vitus's dance, a nervous disorder characterized by involuntary, uncontrollable movements of the body and limbs. This illness put her in the hospital for almost three months, followed by a lengthy recuperation at home. During this period the Dublin schools initiated a strong campaign against the use of alcohol. Because "among the Jewish population drunkenness was almost unheard of," Jessie thought it unnecessary to force the children to take a pledge against drinking.[15] Nevertheless, the temperance message that alcohol "was the devil himself that was in the bottle" caused Jessie to reject her doctor's prescription of "a little whiskey to help stimulate my appetite."[16] Even though the rector of her school encouraged Jessie to follow medical orders, she refused to break her pledge against consuming intoxicating liquor. Jessie's reputation as a strong-willed individual was already well established.

In October 1899, Jessie was physically able to return to school, and she attended classes at Central Model School, larger and more cosmopolitan than St. Peter's. At Central Model, an hour of religious instruction was offered each morning. However, students of less well-represented denominations or non-Christian faiths were excused. Instead, these children assembled in "the classroom assigned to the 'No religion' as we were jokingly called" for a study period.[17] Ignoring the rule for quiet, these students, representative of different religions and cultures, generally spent the time visiting and becoming better acquainted. "I think that was an ideal setting for instilling a feeling of tolerance for the other fellow's beliefs," Jessie later reflected.[18]

The Jewish faith was an integral part of the Spiro home, and even though the Christian religion predominated in Dublin, Jessie never felt discriminated against or isolated because of her beliefs. Her parents taught that all religions should be respected but that Jewish traditions should be upheld.

> Hanukkah in our family was very much of a family holiday. We never went in for parties or extra company, just kept it among ourselves. Naturally there was a lot of Christmas spirit around us, and [it was] carefully explained that we had no reason to celebrate Christmas, but that by concentrating on Hanukkah we could retain our dignity, not by copying our Christian neighbors and having plum pudding or turkey.[19]

Regardless, she had a youthful need for acceptance, and attendance at the annual Hanukkah play, which was traditionally held on a Sunday afternoon, allowed Jessie to feel a unity with her neighbors who observed the Christian Sabbath.

When Jessie was a teenager, relationships with young men caused humiliation when she was "strictly cautioned not to get too friendly with the Gentile boys."[20] Since many of these "nice lads" had been friends from childhood, it was difficult to accept the new rule to limit her associations with them, but, Jessie remembered, "it seems that each time we went out, or even talked to a Gentile lad, after we had grown up, there was an accompanying sense of guilt, which as we grew older did not seem at all worth the effort, so we cut it out."[21]

Jessie finished school at the age of fifteen and went to work for her father in his printing office, where she stayed for six years. In April 1909, her brother Abram, who was working in London, invited Jessie to come for a visit, and while there he suggested that she take a secretarial course and then find a job. She welcomed that challenge, and at the end of the six months of training accepted a position with Cooper Hewitt Co., a firm promoting mercury vapor lights, which she enjoyed until she learned that the women in the firm earned half as much as the men.[22] Concerned about equality, Jessie joined the Women's Freedom League, a pacificist suffrage organization. "It took some courage to announce oneself as a suffragette, and much more to take an active part in the campaign," but her commitment to equal rights for women gave her the strength.[23] "I realized that our absolute faith in the movement was so strong that we felt the world could not progress in any manner unless women were given equal rights."[24] Jessie became intensely devoted to the cause and attended meetings every evening that did not end until almost ten o'clock. Although she had to be in her office at nine the following mornings, she found the work so "stimulating and worthwhile" that she did not object to the busy schedule.[25] On one occasion Jessie helped organize a march in Hyde Park that her mother felt had the potential to turn into a riot. Mrs. Spiro, fearing for her daughter's safety, asked that she not participate, and Jessie complied. Later, recalling that incident, her mother remarked to Bob that "Jessie may have strong ideas, but I've found that you will be able to reason with her."[26] Years later Jessie reflected that:

> The work we did on the platform was to be of great benefit to me in my life in Alaska, as the first bill passed by the Alaska Territorial Legislature, when they got Home Rule in 1912–13, at their first Session, was one granting the women of Alaska equal rights with men. I was thrilled when I heard about it, and though some of the men in Bob's store scoffed at it, remarking that it was just a gag to make it seem that the population was greater than it really was, still that did not dampen my ardor, nor my pleasure in the knowledge that I had come to a country full of opportunity, and had changed from a Subject of King George, to a full fledged citizen of a flour-ishing democracy.[27]

Bob and Jessie married in Ireland on May 17, 1912. On the first of June they set sail for the United States to make their home in Alaska. Pictured here, they honeymooned aboard the *Mauretania* crossing the Atlantic.
(Robert and Jessie Bloom Collection, UAF-1994-0170-00001, Archives, University of Alaska Fairbanks)

On Christmas Eve 1910, Bob Bloom arrived in London from Fairbanks to help settle the estate of his brother, Zelick, who had died a month earlier. While there he and Jessie, who were second cousins, became reacquainted. With Jessie's brother they made a trip to Dublin to visit family, and after a couple of months Bob proposed marriage. Even before she accepted, she gave notice in her office, treated her coworkers to an evening at the theater, cleaned out her desk, and returned to Dublin. There Jessie and Bob shared their decision to marry with family and friends, but because Bob needed to return to Alaska to tend to business and was not prepared to arrive with a wife, he suggested that Jessie remain in Dublin for a year, after which he would return for her and they would marry. One of Bob's motives was for Jessie to learn how to cook and keep house. To facilitate this, he offered to provide Jessie with an allowance so that she did not need to work or rely on her father. Her "flabbergasted" friends nicknamed her the "kept woman."[28] For the next sixteen months Jessie enjoyed taking walks, attending the theater and concerts, and presumably learning domestic skills. Although it would appear she had the time, Jessie did not actively participate in the Dublin suffrage movement. Instead, time with her mother became a cherished memory. "It was during that period that I was able to talk to Mother as an adult and learn more about her background...and best of all of course was the fact that Bob belonged to the same background."[29]

Bob returned to Dublin a year later, and on May 17, 1912, he and Jessie were married in a private Jewish ceremony. On the first of June, with trunks of Irish linens and English silver, Jessie and Bob left the British Isles bound for Alaska. After a leisurely trip across the United States, visiting friends and relatives who had previously immigrated, they boarded the steamer *Dolphin* in Seattle on the Fourth of July and sailed north amid a display of fireworks that lit up the city like a "fairyland." As the landscape faded, Bob and Jessie relaxed.

> Bob was tired and went to our stateroom....I did not want to talk to anyone. I wanted time to myself. I stood near the lifeboats in a secluded part to watch the scenery in the long summer twilight. I know I prayed. I know I was homesick, and I know I had a serious talk to myself, and then I looked up and there were the mountains in all their majesty. I knew I was blessed.[30]

On the voyage up the Inland Passage Jessie met Lena Morrow Lewis, a Socialist Party organizer and the first woman elected to the party's National Executive Committee.[31] In Alaska to garner support of the working class for the fall elections, Lena conversed with Jessie about suffrage and temperance. Although together for only one day and despite Jessie's rejection of formal membership in the Socialist Party, the two women became lifelong friends. Periodically over the years Jessie contributed money to Lena's endeavors, and to the four daughters Jessie would have later "Auntie Lena" became a special friend who sent gifts and letters as she

In 1912, while sailing up the Inland Passage to Alaska, Jessie met Lena Morrow
Lewis (above), a Socialist Party organizer. They became lifelong friends.
(Robert and Jessie Bloom Collection, UAF-1975-0023-00005, Archives, University of Alaska Fairbanks)

Jessie arrived in Fairbanks only a few weeks before this Midnight Sun
Carnival on June 21, in which she undoubtedly participated.
(Robert and Jessie Bloom Collection, UAF-1963-0089-00027, Archives, University of Alaska Fairbanks)

traveled in support of social and political causes. Meta Bloom Buttnick, Jessie's old-
est child, remembered that Lena's "letters used to come in envelopes from different
hotels in different cities so, as she said, we could follow her across the country."[32]

When the ship reached Skagway, Jessie and Bob traveled by White Pass and
Yukon Railway to Whitehorse, where they boarded a steamer for Tanana. The
weeklong journey down the Yukon River in midsummer was an exciting and
romantic experience for Jessie. "We stopped several times each day at wood camps
or fish camps or regular settlements—the continuous daylight made it appear like
one lazy summer day; no routine about resting or eating, just catch as can and
go as you please."[33] On July 19 at five thirty in the morning Jessie caught her first
glimpse of Fairbanks as the steamer maneuvered to the dock. After breakfast and
a visit to his store, Bob took Jessie to a small frame house on Third Avenue and
proudly announced, "This is ours!"[34] Jessie looked around the two small rooms
and declared, "It felt like HOME!"[35] The next morning Bob was awakened at six
o'clock when the Northern Commercial Company whistle blew. He got the stove
going and called, "'Get up Jessie. I have the kettle boiling. I know that a white man
can't talk to you until you have a pot of tea.'"[36] Jessie recalled, "We were acting like
old married people."[37]

That day Jessie had her first social caller, Ruth Condit, wife of the Presbyterian
minister, who invited Jessie to participate in the Presbyterian Ladies' Aid Society.
Mabel Moore stopped in and suggested they take a walk, a daily practice that Jessie
adopted, and in the afternoon Jessie was invited to join some other women for tea.

Fred Musgjerd delivered water to the homes of Fairbanks with his horse-drawn sledge. *(Gaustad Bartlett Collection, UAF-1972-0156-00370, Archives, University of Alaska Fairbanks)*

Her introduction to Fairbanks social life was warm and spontaneous, and Jessie felt genuinely welcomed.

Although Jessie had spent the previous year learning domestic skills, she discovered early that housekeeping in Alaska was quite different from in Dublin. Bob showed her how to use the woodstove for cooking and explained that old potatoes that had sprouted could still be used after "taking the whiskers off."[38] One day a neighbor woman, with gun in hand, stopped by to explain that none of the meat at the butcher's shop looked appealing so she was going down by the river to shoot some ptarmigan for dinner. Quickly Jessie learned that procuring food in Fairbanks was a unique experience.

One of the first social functions that Jessie attended was the Presbyterian Sunday school picnic. While everyone was eating lunch, a little girl came running up to announce that her friend had brought an egg that the chicken had laid. "I was still too recent an arrival from the Outside to be impressed by 'an egg the chicken laid,' but I was soon to find out," Jessie remembered.[39] Eggs were brought in on the last river boat in the fall, and as the seasons changed so did the eggs, until by spring they had a very strong taste. The resourceful women had developed ways to use these eggs without affecting the taste of the food they prepared. Spice cake was a favorite baked good because the cook could disguise the strong taste of the eggs by doubling the amount of spices called for in the recipe. Bob was partial to gingerbread, and Jessie discovered that increasing the spice completely covered the egg taste.

Bob with baby daughter Meta, born April 5, 1913.
(Robert and Jessie Bloom Collection, UAF-1972-0108-00001N,
Archives, University of Alaska Fairbanks)

Jessie also learned methods of shopping and food storage that were foreign to her. Staple foods such as flour, sugar, coffee, shortening, and "the Alaska cow," as evaporated milk was called, were ordered a year in advance. At first it seemed a complicated task to determine how much of what kinds of things would be needed, but Jessie quickly got the system under control and enjoyed the fact that this method of stocking up practically eliminated the complications of shopping. Jessie's back porch became the wintertime freezer, the basement a root cellar and storage place for the bottled fruits and vegetables that she put up at fall harvest time. Large quantities of pies and breads were frozen and stored on the porch, and salmon bellies were pickled and stored in a crock. Moose, sheep, and ptarmigan provided most of the meat, and her first winter Jessie learned that vegetable seeds were started at the end of February in southern exposure windows so that by late May plants were ready to set out in the garden. One year the fall harvest yielded more carrots than Jessie could store in her root cellar, and carrot pudding was the solution. "That winter my desert [*sic*] problem was solved. All I had to do was to break off a chunk of a carrot pudding, and put it in the double boiler early in the morning," where it gradually steamed until ready to be served.[40]

The opening of the Alaska railroad from Seward to Fairbanks in 1923 changed how Fairbanks dealt with its food needs, and Jessie considered it a "luxury beyond the wildest dreams" to be able to get fresh produce in the grocery store only ten days out of Seattle.[41] Although Jessie appreciated the conveniences brought about by improved transportation, she was not always eager to adopt changes, and the electric cooking stove was the most difficult modern convenience for Jessie to accept.

With all its time-saving gadgets, the electric appliance could not compare to a woodstove, which allowed you to keep a pot of water simmering ready for tea and to humidify your house in winter. Food cooked on the woodstove could be started in the morning, and this slow-cooking method filled the house with a pleasant aroma and allowed the cook to take advantage of cheaper and tougher cuts of meat. In addition, the woodstove was the rubbish burner, kept flat irons hot for use whenever needed, and helped warm the house. For Jessie, her woodstove's "live" heat gave "a feeling of what home should be."[42]

During a 1976 interview Jessie was asked if life had been hard in early Fairbanks. "No, it wasn't very hard," Jessie responded. "First of all, Bob didn't expect much and he was very, very helpful. He was helpful with the baby and he was helpful with the housekeeping."[43] Jessie further noted that Fairbanks was a place where people did whatever needed doing regardless of preconceived roles. She recalled one incident when a woman who had just finished scrubbing the Masonic Hall floor showed Jessie the seventy-five-dollar dress she planned to wear to that night's dance. Jessie questioned what kind of place was Fairbanks if the women who get down on their hands and knees to scrub floors buy expensive dresses and attend the balls. Certainly this was a different set of values than she was used to, but the experience was a good introduction to the less structured frontier.[44]

In the spring of 1913, before Jessie had been in Fairbanks a year, she gave birth to a daughter, named Meta for Bob's grandmother. Dissatisfied with a male doctor she had visited in early pregnancy, Jessie sought out Aline Bradley, the only female doctor in town, to deliver her. Meta was born April 5 at St. Matthew's Episcopal Hospital, and two days later the *Fairbanks Daily News-Miner* announced her arrival on the front page.[45] The following Sunday the Episcopal Church choir came in to sing hymns, and Jessie commented to the rector that she "liked the idea of my little Episcopalian Jewess being greeted by music so early after her arrival."[46] Shortly after the birth of her first child, Jessie was pregnant again, but at Bob's insistence she made arrangements to go to Dublin for this child's birth. Before departing, however, Jessie had the opportunity to participate in one of Fairbanks' greatest celebrations.

Fairbanksans never missed a chance to have a party, and the impending passage of the Alaska Railroad Bill in February 1914 provided good reason to celebrate. Spirits were high as people believed that almost fifty years after the purchase of Alaska from the Russians, year-round transportation into the Interior was imminent. In anticipation of the growth and development that was surely to come, the Fraternal Order of Eagles arranged for a "Hard Times" ball to be held on Friday, February 13. Dress for the occasion, which the *Fairbanks Daily News-Miner* predicted would be "one of the grandest events of the Fairbanks social season," was restricted to overalls, calico gowns, and rags. "White collars and dress suits are absolutely barred," the newspaper warned.[47] To encourage appropriate costumes, the Eagles offered prizes to the poorest-dressed man and woman in attendance. W. F. Thompson, editor of the *News-Miner*, predicted the bill would pass in Congress, which would ensure the expenditure of forty million dollars in the territory. He urged community spirit by suggesting:

> Let's spend a portion of that $40,000,000 in advance. It is guaranteed by the United States government and is sure to come to us, and the bulk of it will be paid out through the First National Bank of this city. We can collect in good time, even though we are compelled to use strong-arm methods. Let's celebrate![48]

On February 18, inch-high headlines in the newspaper informed readers that "BILL PASSES" by a vote of 230 to 87. An advertisement announced that James Wickersham, Alaska's delegate to Congress, was celebrating that evening at the Washington Hotel, and the community was invited to join him and express their gratitude for his hard work that secured the passage of the bill. When the N.C. Company whistle blew, signaling passage of the bill, "hats began to fly in the air and flags began to appear at the windows of the offices and in front of the business houses."[49] One resident was so excited about the event that he "raised the electric lighted picture of Delegate Wickersham to the top of his flag staff."[50] Wickersham was sure that a railroad would improve the sagging economy, and Fairbanks civic and social organizations echoed his sentiments and immediately pledged money in support of the grand celebration, which Thompson predicted would last a week or longer. Half-fare train rides in from the creeks were offered by the Tanana Valley Railroad to lure the miners into town.

Plans complete, the celebration began at noon on Monday, February 23, with a parade through the downtown streets, and an evening torchlight parade was followed by a masked ball at the Eagles Hall. The *News-Miner* encouraged everyone "to get all of the confetti obtainable and to make as much noise as is possible as horns and other noisemakers are to be had cheap."[51] Specially appointed deputies were in place to maintain order, but Thompson assured celebrants that "they will in no way effect [*sic*] the hilarity and feeling of good fellowship which is sure to prevail, being only for the purpose of preventing absolutely lawless acts."[52] To heighten the excitement, Gordon's Store advertised a special fifty-dollar rate for a round-trip ticket on the "First Big Railroad Excursion, Sept. 2, 1916," and private businesses, school, and government offices announced they would close at noon on Monday.[53] Anticipating a large number of advertisers, Thompson urged businesses to get their ad copy in early because "there are four able-bodied celebrators in the *News-Miner* office" who want to participate in the festivities.[54] By all accounts, the celebration surpassed expectations.

The day after the party, Thompson wrote what must have been his shortest, most subdued ever editorial. He stated simply that,

> last night's celebration was SOME celebration. When we look around our office and see one sober man attempting to get out a newspaper all by himself, we realize that the *News-Miner* bunch must have celebrated with the re[s]t of them.... For the sins of omission and commission in this issue, good people, forgive us! However, the way we feel about it just now, we don't give a hang whether you forgive us or not.[55]

For all the fanfare and apparent fun had in connection with the passage of the Railroad Bill, Jessie Bloom remembered a sober side in the aftermath. During the partying, the town was thrown wide open, and because everyone was in masquerade people were disguised. This allowed women to enter bars and walk "The Row," two areas of town ordinarily off-limits to them. Because the celebrating went on into the night, husbands and wives with children took turns staying home and attending the festivities. With all the drinking and the freedom offered by the masks, some people engaged in behavior that they probably would not consider under more scrutinized conditions. When recalling this event, Jessie remarked that "the 'Girls' [from the Row] were in the masquerade also, and from reports that subsequently came in, they were the most ladylike of all those who took part in the dancing and general merrymaking."[56] A few days later when people realized how

Children riding a horse-drawn parade float in 1914. The Bloom girls
rode a similar float in 1923 at the railroad celebration parade.
(James M. Whitely Collection, UAF-1974-0095-00057, Archives, University of Alaska Fairbanks)

much money they had spent and how foolishly they had acted, many decided to
take action to prevent any similar celebration from occurring in Fairbanks. Some
of the women "who had imbibed not wisely but too well" organized themselves
into the Fourth Division Drys, the group that was instrumental in Fairbanks for
the passage of the temperance laws two years later.[57] The town's commitment to
more subdued celebration apparently was sincere. It was not until Thanksgiving
1918 that Fairbanksans turned out for such a wild time when a community dance
was advertised as "the biggest Masquerade since the Railroad Ball."[58]

As soon as the confetti settled, the women of Fairbanks discussed their responsibility as voters and organized the Women's Civic Club. Because there had been
little debate the year before regarding the passage of the women's suffrage bill by
the Alaska Territorial Legislature, many women felt unfamiliar with how local
politics worked and what the issues were for the next election. The Civic Club
provided an educational forum and allowed the women jointly to nominate the
first woman to run for elected office.[59] Nominated for clerk of the school board
was Anna Zimmerman, an educator who had graduated from Blackburn College
in Illinois and done graduate work at the University of Chicago and Bryn Mawr
and who had come to Fairbanks in 1908 with her mining engineer husband, John.
The Civic Club believed they had made a good choice, and the voters elected her
to serve for several terms.[60]

In July 1914, Jessie and fourteen-month-old Meta traveled to Ireland to await the birth of the Blooms' second child. On December 6, as the Germans bombed the British port of Yarmouth, Deborah Bloom was born and named for Jessie's grandmother. The next two years were "a time of deep despair to many people in Ireland."[61] Some Irish wanted home rule, which would have allowed the country to remain part of Britain but with its own parliament and domestic autonomy. The British Parliament passed the Home Rule Bill in 1914, but the outbreak of the First World War prevented it from taking effect. An extreme nationalist faction, the Irish Republican Brotherhood, formed in favor of complete independence for an Irish republic. This force opposed Britain's idea to draft young Irish men into military service, and by 1916 the disagreement had peaked and the Irish Republicans staged the Easter Monday Rebellion in an effort to establish their own provisional government. The rebellion was doomed to fail before it started due to the inadequate strength of the Irish forces, and Jessie could not sympathize with the Republicans, who, she believed, "were holding on to a grievance of a couple of hundred years."[62] Although the Easter Monday Rebellion ultimately led to Irish independence, historian Joe McCarthy wrote that at the time most of Ireland, agreeing with Jessie, viewed the destruction and bloodshed with glum indifference or irritation, "regarding the whole performance as a reckless and unnecessary outburst by a few hotheaded political fanatics."[63] Jessie resented the "bedlam" caused by the rebellion. Conversation was guarded, people were forced to remain indoors to avoid sniper fire, and homes were searched by the British at gunpoint. She was relieved to leave Dublin in June 1916, after two years, for her return to America.

The journey on board the *New York* from Liverpool to the United States was tense due to the hostilities of war-torn Europe. Jessie feared floating mines, and even though the passengers had been assured that the ship's American flag protected it from attack, she was ill at ease. For the first several nights she sat in the cabin, fully clothed and ever alert, watching her two children sleep. In New York Jessie and the girls were met by friends with whom they planned to spend a couple of weeks in Connecticut. Jessie finally relaxed for the first time since beginning the journey. However, an outbreak of polio in New York caused Jessie to cut short her visit and head to Seattle for her trip back to Alaska. It was a welcome relief to board the Alaska Steamship vessel that headed north. "The moment I came aboard friends from Fairbanks and those going there identified themselves and we immediately became good company."[64] Finally, in August, Jessie and the girls were met at the dock by Bob as they returned home to Fairbanks. This was the first of many nostalgic returns to Alaska, and Jessie remarked that she always had a feeling of "coming home" when she stepped back on Alaska soil.[65]

Years later Deborah's birthplace caused jealousy among the Bloom girls. In 1923, when Fairbanks celebrated the opening of the railroad from Seward to the Interior, a float ridden by the Native Sons and Daughters of the Golden North, an organization created to recognize children of pioneers who were born in the North, was part of a large parade. Because Deborah was ineligible for membership, she watched dejectedly as her three sisters, all born in Fairbanks, donned starched white dresses in readiness. Mournfully Debbie asked her mother, "Why did you have to go to Dublin to born me?"[66]

Bob delighted in the reunion of his family, and proudly showed them all of the home improvements made during their absence. Not only did the house have a new kitchen, it had its own well and pump, a bathroom, a sink in the kitchen, and running hot and cold water. It was late August and the annual grocery order, which Bob had placed, arrived. The quantity of food caused Jessie to feel a sense of gratitude for the abundance so close at hand. Contrasted to shortages she had experienced during the previous two years in Dublin, life in Alaska was one of plenty. Jessie felt indescribable joy for her family and Alaska—her home.

Grateful to be back in Fairbanks, Jessie did not object that she "had to use elbow grease" to benefit from the plenty.[67] The hard work allowed her a good night's sleep and a sense of self-satisfaction. Supplies were readily available, gardening, berry picking, and hunting provided food, and large timber resources furnished logs for homes and fuel to heat them. Families had fun together cutting ice out of the river for home refrigeration, and Jessie knew cabin fever could be avoided by taking a daily walk regardless of the weather conditions. "Even the act of getting dressed to go outdoors was a morale booster," she remembered.[68] Jessie also realized that the two years she had spent in Dublin had helped her "to grow up and to appreciate Bob," and the experience gave her the "opportunity to make a new life with him."[69]

The winter of 1916–17 sped by, and on May 28 Jessie gave birth to her third daughter, named Olga after her mother. The Fairbanks economy was at "low ebb" that spring, caused by many men leaving for the war. Mining efforts were curtailed, and "business was practically at a standstill."[70] Managing meager resources occupied much of Jessie's time, and her social life centered around sharing money-saving strategies with other women. Embroidered and hemmed flour sacks served as curtains, aprons, pillow cases, and dish towels. Instead of purchasing water, families used barrels to catch gallons of rain for home use, and some residents even reused coffee grounds.[71] This climate prevailed until Jessie's fourth child, Ruth, was born September 18, 1918.

Like her own mother, Jessie took an active role in guiding the young minds of her daughters and other children. In 1918, with direction from Florence Smith Kelley, a primary-school teacher, Jessie formed a small kindergarten composed of six children. The youngsters met daily at the Bloom home for two hours in the afternoon, learned sight-reading and paper-cutting techniques, and occupied their time with other preschool activities. To improve her knowledge and teaching skills, Jessie enrolled in a correspondence course sponsored by the Bureau of

Bob Bloom's store was a gathering place for local men—an
"intellectual delicatessen," according to one of Jessie's friends.
(Robert and Jessie Bloom Collection, UAF-1994-0170-00007, Archives, University of Alaska Fairbanks)

Education in Washington, D.C., which led to her certification as a kindergarten teacher in 1921.[72] To help the program, Bob procured a secondhand gramophone and records for the students' use. When Jessie realized that some of the lyrics to the songs were risqué, she queried Bob about the origin of the material, and he confessed that he had bought the equipment from "one of the 'sporting girls.'"[73] Jessie admitted that overall the original owner had very good taste in music, and most of the records were integrated into her curriculum.

The settlement of Graehl was across the Chena Slough from the town of Fairbanks, and in May 1919, Jessie began taking her daughters, the kindergarten pupils, and any other children who wished to go over for picnics. Many of the prospectors, trappers, and woodsmen had cabins there, and on their first trip they met Sam Jensen, who had a carpenter shop. Meta immediately recognized him as one of the men who frequented Bob's store, and Jessie accepted Sam's invitation to use his hot water or his stove if they had need. On future trips Sam allowed the girls to help themselves to the produce in his garden, and when he noticed how much they enjoyed picking and eating the fresh peas and carrots, he planted a garden just for them the following year. The girls developed a special friendship with Sam that lasted for many years.

During these outings, Jessie and the girls were intrigued by the varieties of mushrooms that grew in Graehl, but they hesitated to pick any because they could not identify which ones were poisonous. In 1923, *National Geographic* published an article about mushrooms that helped the girls make identification. Interest in gathering specimens spread to the Graehl residents, who fondly referred to this as Jessie's "mushroom project."[74] Jessie formed classes to identify and collect specimens, and she developed a recipe for pickled puffballs that found its way into the Episcopal Ladies' Guild cookbook. That year the Tanana Valley fair provided a mushroom exhibit, and Jessie's girls entered twenty different specimens. By 1950, the exhibit had grown to more than forty.[75]

The kindergarten provided Jessie with a benefit beyond her love of children. Because other mothers accompanied the group on outings, Jessie did not have to devote her constant attention to watching the children. One picnic in the summer of 1919 had the advantage of freeing Jessie, if only momentarily, from day-to-day cares:

> It was way past seven and the sun was still high in the sky. I suddenly realized that there would be no night, and that I was in Alaska. I no longer was under pressure to attend to the children, the household, Bob or any other thing. I could actually sit out in the clear pure unpolluted Alaska air and think....I had time to feel the wonderful closeness with the Infinite.[76]

In spite of the previous leisurely summer, the spring of 1920 was particularly difficult for Jessie. Four young children demanded most of her time and energy, and because of Bob's fear of house fires he did not want babysitters until the youngest daughter was old enough to take care of herself and escape in case of an emergency. Even though Bob often watched the children, Jessie was frequently housebound. Typically, Bob left for work at seven in the morning and did not return home until after ten at night. His store was a gathering place for the local men to share their news and discuss popular issues affecting the community and the territory—an "intellectual delicatessen" according to Jessie's close friend Mary Lee Davis.[77] When Bob returned home, he was full of interesting conversation, while Jessie could respond only with a litany of child-related and domestic activities. She felt deprived of adult-oriented mental stimulation and eagerly accepted Mary Lee's invitation to meet weekly, when their husbands attended Masonic Lodge meetings, to indulge in reading and discussing good books. Mary Lee, educated at Wellesley and Radcliffe, enjoyed the challenges of a successful writing career, and her background in literature added depth to the Wednesday-evening study sessions that she and Jessie shared for the next three years.

The year 1923 was a turning point for Fairbanks. Then twenty years old, the community had already outlived its projected life span, and technological advances pointed to increased longevity. The railroad began operation in 1923 when President Harding drove the "Golden Spike," and the Alaska Agricultural College, opened in 1922, was growing. Additional mining opportunities were available, and aviation had captured the entrepreneurial spirit of many pioneers. Fairbanks prospered, and new residents arrived regularly when the Fairbanks Exploration

During World War II the Bloom home served as a social and spiritual center for Jewish servicemen in the area. Bob (back to camera) conducting a religious service.
(Robert and Jessie Bloom Collection, UAF-1963-0089-00133, Archives, University of Alaska Fairbanks)

Jessie (left) and the Fairbanks postmaster admire the Juliette postage
stamp commemorating the founding
of the Girl Scouts, 1948.
(Robert and Jessie Bloom Collection,
UAF-1975-0023-00008, Archives,
University of Alaska Fairbanks)

Company established itself. Although Jessie was pleased with the community's growth and proud of her role in its development, she needed a break from the short days and cold temperatures of a Fairbanks winter. Because of Bob's commitments as a regent at the college, his part ownership of the Fairbanks Aviation Company, and his own business to run, he could not leave the community. However, at his suggestion in September 1923, Jessie and the girls boarded the train for Seward, where they met the steamer to take them to Seattle for the winter.

Once in Seattle the girls quickly settled into their routines, and Jessie found a place to live in a Jewish neighborhood, which offered participation in synagogue activities, something they had never experienced in Fairbanks. Although Bob and Jessie taught their children the orthodox religion, and the family observed all Jewish holidays, Fairbanks had only a few Jewish families and the girls had never benefited from close association with a group that shared the same heritage. (It was 1939 before regular Jewish worship services were held in Fairbanks.[78]) The move was also Jessie's first experience living in America outside of Alaska. Seattle's climate, lovely green trees, and its proximity to the sea all reminded her of Dublin. She quickly forgot the continuous struggles of life in Alaska, and memory of the work involved in preparing for freeze-up and the months of snow and cold paled now that she was surrounded by lush vegetation. Life in Seattle seemed completely remote from Fairbanks, but because Bob's reputation as a well-respected business-

Jessie and Bob after High Holy
Day Services, September 3, 1943.
(Robert and Jessie Bloom Collection,
UAF-1980-0084-00001, Archives,
University of Alaska Fairbanks)

man extended to Seattle, Jessie regularly met people with connections to Alaska
who knew him.

One evening while Jessie and the girls were taking a walk, they saw roller skates
for sale in a shop window. The girls each wanted a pair, but Jessie explained she had
spent all her money at the market so the purchase would have to wait. Meta, who
recognized the name of the business, remarked that she thought Bob traded with
this firm. In walked Jessie with the four girls trailing behind. She introduced herself and said, "My daughter tells me that she knows that Bob has an account here.
I would like to get skates for the girls."[79] Jessie and the girls left with four pairs!

Jessie had hoped that Bob would join the family for a vacation during their
stay in Seattle, but demands at home kept him in Alaska. Regardless, the children
enjoyed their associations, and Jessie benefited from an orthodox Jewish congrega-
tion to instill the traditional religious values in her daughters. She maintained a
kosher kitchen and adhered to all religious practices and traditions. However, by
the summer of 1925, Jessie felt it was time to return to Fairbanks, and she and the
girls arrived in August after a two-year absence.

Bob met his family at the train depot and took them to their new home—a surprise to Jessie. It was a beautiful two-story house with hardwood floors and a con-
crete basement, but Jessie "just cried!!! I was so frustrated!...I think what upset
me most was the subconscious thought that with a home like that I would be stuck

Jessie and her four daughters, 1934. Back row standing, left to right:
Olga Bloom Bakker, Ruth Bloom Ibbetson. Seated, left to right: Deborah
Bloom Kaplan, Jessie Spiro Bloom, Meta Bloom Buttnick.
(Robert and Jessie Bloom Collection, UAF-1994-0170-00006N, Archives, University of Alaska Fairbanks)

in Fairbanks indefinitely."[80] Clearly Jessie was conflicted about wanting to be part of the exciting and history-making frontier and at the same time wanting a comfortable life in a more temperate urban environment. After she calmed down, Bob explained that when a previous resident left town the mortgage to his house ended up in Bob's hands. He hired some carpenters to dismantle it and salvage whatever they could to put into the new Bloom house a few doors away from their previous residence. Handsome windows with beveled panes and the spiral staircase came from the demolished house, and the hardwood floor was purchased from the old dance hall when it was torn down. Jessie had to admit that it was beautiful, and she busied herself making it into their home.

That fall Jessie organized the first Girl Scout troop in Fairbanks as an outgrowth of the Sunday school at the Presbyterian Church. The girls and their parents, as well as the "whole town [were] willing and anxious to get back of our movement."[81] Activities that first winter centered around sewing, cooking, and weekly hiking. While out on one hike the girls heard an airplane flying overhead. Knowing that Ben Eielson and Sir Hubert Wilkins were overdue on a flight, the girls hustled to the local airfield, arriving just in time to see the pioneer aviators

Jessie walking down a Seattle street.
(Robert and Jessie Bloom Collection, UAF-1963-0089-00140, Archives, University of Alaska Fairbanks)

land. Jessie later recorded that "our girls were extremely proud to think that their Troop had been the first" to greet the lost aviators.[82]

By spring 1926, the girls decided to organize a camp for themselves at Birch Lake, sixty miles south of Fairbanks on the road to Valdez. To raise money the scouts produced an amateur talent show on June 21 and profited enough to pay the transportation costs for twenty girls to attend camp that August. When the camping experience ended, Jessie filed a report to ensure that their activity was registered with the Girl Scout headquarters. In answer to a question regarding their milk supply, Jessie noted that they had taken canned milk. A special note mentioned an outstanding show of the northern lights that had occurred toward the end of the camp. Some time later an article appeared in the national Girl Scout bulletin that amply noted the scouts' use of canned milk but, to Jessie's disappointment, neglected mention of the northern lights.

The next winter the troop focused on singing, art and handicraft classes, and hiking. That summer the girls held their second camp at Birch Lake and began a wildflower project that was similar to the mushroom project initiated some years before. A tourist from Chicago donated fifty dollars for prize money to the fair committee to encourage interest. The Girl Scouts collected, classified, and mounted specimens, which they exhibited at the 1929 fair, and several prizes in this division went to the scouts.

When word spread that Alaska had a Girl Scout troop, letters arrived periodically from Outside requesting Alaska pen pals. However, the girls were not interested in corresponding because, as Jessie explained, "the letters were usually couched in terms that plainly showed that they had such an erroneous idea of Alaska. It would have been too difficult to explain that we were white folks, lived in houses, had electric lights etc."[83]

Jessie continued to lead the Girl Scout program for the next three years. On one of her visits to Fairbanks in the late 1960s, Jessie remarked, "Scouting has come a long way since our day."[84] By 1985, the sixtieth anniversary of the Farthest North Girl Scout Council, the scouting program in Fairbanks had grown from one troop to 112, with more than one thousand registered participants.

In 1928, the Bloom girls ranged in age from ten to fifteen, and Jessie felt they should experience a more traditional environment. She decided to return to Dublin, where she believed more opportunities existed for their cultural, academic, religious, and social development. She was absent from Fairbanks for almost a decade before feeling that her children were on secure paths.

When Jessie returned to Fairbanks in 1937, it was the first time in almost twenty-five years that she and Bob had lived alone. Jessie hoped Bob would sell the store and retire so they could settle permanently in Seattle, but he was reluctant to give up his business and community activities. Any consideration to Jessie's request was thwarted a few years later when, at the outbreak of World War II,

Bob celebrating Rosh Hashanah, 1950s.
(Robert and Jessie Bloom Collection, UAF-1963-0089-00139, Archives, University of Alaska Fairbanks)

Bob was asked by the Jewish Welfare Board to accept the position of lay rabbi for Interior Alaska. Without hesitation, both Bob and Jessie responded that their home would serve as the social and spiritual headquarters for Jewish servicemen stationed near or traveling through Fairbanks. "The Blooms' hospitality became legendary among the Jewish servicemen," Rabbi Eisenberg wrote in his history of Jews in Alaska.[85]

In 1950, Jessie at last got her wish to leave Alaska when she and Bob bought a house on Puget Sound in Seattle. Her desires and expectations for her daughters also came to fruition: two became medical doctors; one a linguist; the other an architect. All four women married Jewish men.

Bob died on April 3, 1974, at age ninety-five, and Jessie passed away November 22, 1980, one month shy of her ninety-third birthday. Both of them are buried at Bikur Cholim-Machzikay Hadath Cemetery in Seattle.

Jessie created a life for herself and her family in Fairbanks based on the European Orthodox Jewish faith and family traditions experienced during her childhood in Dublin. Like her own mother, Jessie fostered in her four daughters

Jessie in early 1980 in Seattle.
(Robert and Jessie Bloom Collection, UAF-1975-23-7, Archives, University of Alaska Fairbanks)

a reverence for learning, community service, and religious observation. With this foundation, Jessie became a woman with intense pride who considered it part of her responsibility to help shape Fairbanks into a stable and productive community. Today, she is remembered as the founder of the Girl Scout program in Fairbanks and by people who knew her as a caring woman committed to nurturing her own and other children.

Jessie left an extensive written record of her life in Alaska—a life of tradition, a life of contrast. Much of her work was prepared beginning in 1951 at the request of Stanley Chyet and Jacob Marcus, archivists at the American Jewish Archives in Cincinnati, Ohio, who encouraged Jessie to create a record of her recollections on topics ranging from day-to-day life in early Fairbanks to her reactions at being Jewish in a predominantly gentile frontier community. Jessie eagerly complied, explaining that it was a "must to get our Alaskan experiences on paper."[86] Even as she submitted monographs and two lengthy memoirs to the repository during the subsequent fourteen years, she frequently lamented that she did not think anyone would be interested in her experiences, and she often questioned that others would find historical significance in what she considered important.

In fact, Jessie's memoirs provide an invaluable glimpse into Alaska social history. The overall theme of her recollections is her pride at being a pioneer in a frontier community. She was challenged and invigorated by the opportunity to participate in the making of history and to live a life that she believed released her from the bonds of conformity of her more sophisticated European background, even though she continually worked to instill traditional social and religious values in her family.

A close reading of her work, however, indicates that as the years passed Jessie was no longer interested in the struggles of life on the frontier, favoring a more temperate climate and an organized society. For instance, by 1951 clearly she had lost her awe for old-timers who had forged a life in Fairbanks and continued to reside in the community. Instead, she chided them as "never seeming to have enough ambition to go Outside."[87] For Jessie, life in Fairbanks seemed to change from one of excitement to one of frustration and endurance, and she responded by absenting herself from Alaska as often as she could.

On the other hand, her husband seemed to flourish in the newness of Fairbanks, where he seized the opportunity to develop a successful business and to participate in the development of the community and the territory. Although the Blooms experienced lengthy separations, they apparently understood each other's needs. By the time Bob and Jessie celebrated their fiftieth wedding anniversary, they had been apart for over a quarter of their married life, but they maintained a solid relationship based on love, respect, and shared tradition. In late 1979, Jessie remarked to friends, "Time marches on and it will be six years in April since Bob left. Somehow the years have been slow in going."[88] Clearly Bob was an integral part of Jessie's existence. As was the Fairbanks experience.

A year and a half before she died, Jessie learned that the Blooms' original Fairbanks house likely would be demolished. She reminisced to Babe and Ted Lowell of Fairbanks about her years in the North and the significance of that house when she wrote that her home's "spirit lives on in the friends, family, and relations who passed through its portals. How many came to our door looking for comfort and always got it? And we got it doubly by being able to relate. All through the years from July 1912 I felt it part of me. I loved it, still do, and even today its memories brings [sic] comfort to me."[89]

Studio portrait of Sarah Margaret Keenan Harrais taken in Salt Lake City
shortly before she moved to Alaska.
(Harrais Family Papers, Box 8, Folder 128, Archives, University of Alaska Fairbanks)

4

Sarah Margaret Keenan Harrais
1872–1964

*And now let us consider what manner of women
we shall endeavor to be,
to the end that the world may find in us
the inspiration of which it is so sorely in need.*[1]

Margaret Harrais

A S A YOUNG GIRL growing up in southeastern Ohio, Margaret Keenan dreamed of mountain vistas and the wide unfenced land of the West in the same way her Scotch-Irish ancestors had envisioned America. When she arrived in Fairbanks in 1916 to become the superintendent of schools, she was no stranger to Alaska or life on the American frontier. "I seem to have a few extra drops of pioneering blood in my veins," she recounted years later.[2] This yearning for new experiences challenged Margaret to leave the familiarity of her childhood and move west in search of new adventures as a teacher first in Idaho, then in Alaska. Family and friends were somewhat skeptical about her move in 1914 to the southeastern Alaska town of Skagway, but it was not removed far enough from civilization to cause alarm. However, her decision, a couple of years later, to relocate to the isolated Interior gold camp of Fairbanks caused concern. Undaunted, she drew on her admiration for other hardy and fearless pioneers, focused her goals, and created a life full of remarkable experiences. Half a century as an educator, a leader in the Woman's Christian Temperance Union (WCTU), a U.S. commissioner, and deputy magistrate for Alaska all provided abundant raw material from which to create vivid portraits of the North.

The next to youngest of seven children, Sarah Margaret was born to Thomas and Martha Reed Keenan on September 23, 1872, on a large farm in Batesville, Ohio. Margaret's intellectual appetite was fed by her father, a Meadville College graduate who had taught school before turning to agriculture.[3] As a child, she eavesdropped on her father's political discussions with friends, eagerly listened to

The sophomore class at Nampa High School, near Boise, Idaho, where Margaret taught in the late 1890s. Margaret is standing far right in the back row.
(Harrais Family Papers, Box 8, Folder 128, Archives, University of Alaska Fairbanks)

him read aloud classic literature to the family, and readily accepted his instruction in support of temperance.[4] After graduating with honors from Batesville High School in 1888, Margaret taught school for several years at Bridgeport, Ohio, before entering Northern Indiana Normal School, where she completed the "scientific" course in 1896.[5] Ready to launch her career on the American frontier, this young woman with an enviable complexion, fine figure, and curly brown hair accepted a position as superintendent of schools for Custer County, Idaho, and moved west. After eight years Margaret returned to Indiana to further her education, earning a B.S. degree from Valparaiso University in 1906, and then moved back to Idaho to continue her career as a school administrator.[6]

Brought up in an environment of decorum and industrial advancement, Margaret experienced some initial discomfort when exposed to a less structured society in an undeveloped region. Her complaint that Idaho was without most modern conveniences including telegraph and telephone resulted in reproach from the old-timers, and her discovery that the railroad did not extend into the area where she lived caused momentary temptation to return to the comforts of her familiar home. Margaret was accustomed to eastern fashion that dictated long dresses down to her ankles and the practice of modestly crossing her ankles, "but never, no never one knee over the other."[7] This etiquette also prescribed that ladies did not go out unchaperoned, but shortly after her arrival in Idaho, Margaret found herself alone riding in a stagecoach with a man she did not even know. Her mind made up to

Margaret's official Woman's Christian Temperance Union photograph, ca. 1915.
(Harrais Family Papers, Box 3/7, Folder 5, Archives, University of Alaska Fairbanks)

succeed in her venture, Margaret quickly learned two lessons of the frontier: "no one is interested in what they do back home," and to fit in she had to accept a new set of standards regarding day-to-day life and behavior.[8] Obviously she adapted to her surroundings because a few years later she bragged that she could "ride like a cowboy and shoot off the heads of rattlesnakes with a six shooter."[9] She also dis-covered, however, that certain principles cannot be violated.

Fairbanks women gather at the George C. Thomas Library for a Woman's Christian
Temperance Union program presented by Cornelia Templeton Hatcher, the president
of the Alaska Chapter of the WCTU, April 16, 1916. Margaret Keenan is fourth from
left standing on the sidewalk. Cornelia is fifth from left standing next to Margaret.
(Courtesy of Frances E. Willard Memorial Library, Evanston, Illinois)

As a young, attractive, and spirited woman it could be expected that Margaret
enjoyed attention from men, and one of these suitors became her husband. On
May 30, 1900, Margaret married George Leonard McGowan in Challis, Idaho;
however, he is never mentioned in her papers or memoirs, and Margaret does not
indicate for how long they were married.[10] She does make it clear that her decision
to abstain from alcoholic beverages and her commitment to the WCTU was in
direct conflict with her husband's desire to open a liquor establishment in Challis.
Margaret offered him the choice of "his bar and liquor store, or her," but when
he explained that the business was too lucrative to ignore, she divorced him and
resumed her maiden name.[11]

After a few more years at Idaho's Nampa High School as a teacher and administrator, and three years in Boise as a clerk in the United States assay office, Margaret was ready to move on. The fond memory of a summer trip in 1902 to Skagway
and Sitka, Alaska, with her older sister, Martha, had not faded. Coupled with this
recollection was her belief that people are "divided into two classes, those who go
and those who stay."[12] As one of the "goers" looking for a new challenge, Margaret
could not resist the tug toward the mysteries of the North. She later remembered

that "Alaska was all beginnings. That was the lure that brought me to Alaska and has kept me contented here through many years."[13] In 1914, she accepted the position as principal of schools in Skagway, where she is credited with starting a parent-teacher association and, with school board approval, initiating the WCTU school savings plan that taught children the concepts of thrift and financial planning.[14] The *Union Signal*, the official publication of the WCTU, reported that under Margaret's guidance the children made the first deposit in the newly established Bank of Alaska when they opened an account with eighty-five dollars.[15] During her tenure in Skagway, Margaret also participated in the first Territorial Convention of the WCTU in May 1915, at which she was elected vice president of the organization for Alaska.[16]

During the summer of 1916, the nation geared up for general elections, and prohibition was a major issue debated across the country. In her capacity as a territorial leader for the WCTU, Margaret accompanied Cornelia Templeton Hatcher, president of Alaska's chapter, on a speaking tour into the Interior. The women arrived in Fairbanks at the end of June and spent three weeks urging residents to vote for prohibition. Although Margaret was not considered the primary lecturer, she addressed and apparently impressed a special meeting of the Women's Civic Club. Before she could leave, the Fairbanks School Board extended to her an unsolicited offer to accept the position of superintendent of schools at an annual salary of $2,475.[17] Later Hatcher reported that this appointment was "significant of the attitude of the fathers and mothers of the North toward the ideals and character of those to whom they would intrust the training of their children."[18]

The day before the announcement of Margaret's appointment, W. F. Thompson, editor of the *Fairbanks Daily News-Miner*, used his column to respond to Mrs. Hatcher's invitation for a face-to-face debate. An antiprohibitionist, Thompson accused Hatcher of being a quasi-Alaskan because she and her husband usually wintered in Seattle and further chided that she had "nothing worth debating."[19] Dubbed by Hatcher the "Booze Bugler of Fairbanks,"[20] Thompson continued his diatribe by stating that her "letters are the same old prohibition stuff, written years ago and mimeographed for constant delivery by every woman who has a pleasing appearance and a good voice and who is willing to desert her home and her husband and tramp about the country on a salary of $15.00 a month."[21] Somehow Margaret escaped Thompson's attack.

Founded in Cleveland, Ohio, in November 1874, the WCTU was established by women concerned with strengthening the values that families represented and emphasizing the home as the center of society. Their points of focus were the abolition of liquor and tobacco, the end of prostitution, and, later, the advent of women's rights. More than forty special departments of the WCTU assigned a member in each chapter the responsibility of working on a specific problem. Prevention was considered a goal, and targeting children in the schoolroom became their arena.

Margaret later philosophized that she "never did have much hope of reforming middle-aged people, but there are measureless possibilities in the children."[22] Through the use of *The Temperance Lesson Book*, a text sponsored by the WCTU and sanctioned as part of the American public school curriculum, America's youth were introduced to the physical and social effects associated with drinking, smoking, and careless sexual activity. A leading nineteenth-century women's organization, the WCTU adopted "program concerns ranging far beyond narrow temperance goals," and its membership "found temperance the most congenial cause through which to increase their involvement in public life."[23] Thus, temperance was the symbolic medium for social change, not simply the message.

In her professional capacity Margaret was strategically placed to advance the WCTU platform, and in the election-day edition of the *News-Miner* Thompson, who apparently continued to ignore Margaret's affiliation with the WCTU, unwittingly gave credence to what she was doing in the schools to further the organization's cause. Thompson reported that at a reception held a few days prior Margaret urged the one hundred parents in attendance to support her belief that:

> schools of today are made up of but two classes; home-makers and home-providers of tomorrow. The school girls of today are the mothers and home-makers of tomorrow, and the school boys are the fathers and home-providers of the future.... [Their] whole education should be with that end in view.[24]

On November 9, Thompson's newspaper reported that Alaska voters had cast their ballots almost two to one for prohibition. To further document that Thompson did not include Margaret in his antiprohibition campaign, he remarked in his November 16 editorial that although he favored the "wet" laws, he believed in women's rights and their participation in government, and although he doubted she would accept, he boldly stated that Margaret should be elected to the city council.

Margaret was undoubtedly pleased with the election results, although the passage of prohibition threatened her chosen profession because, as she told a *Union Signal* reporter, "the public schools of Alaska were supported by revenue from the liquor traffic."[25] With prohibition to go into effect January 1, 1918, funding for education became a crucial concern. Prior to the Treaty of Cession, the Russian Church funded education heavily, and, according to former state legislator Niilo Koponen's history of education in Alaska, "until 1905 the Russian Orthodox Church spent more money on education in Alaska than did the American government."[26] This reality—combined with the knowledge that the first schools in Alaska after the American purchase in 1867 were established, funded, and operated by American churches—caused many Alaskans to become discontented with this perceived "un-American mixing of Church and State."[27] The termination of Russian philanthropy in 1917 coupled with the impending loss of saloon and liquor-license fee revenue due to the passage of prohibition threatened Alaska's educational system.

Alaska Territorial Governor J.F. A. Strong signs the Prohibition Bill which took effect in early 1918. Left to right: Representative C.K. Snow, author of the bill; Governor J.F.A. Strong (seated); Senator B.F. Millard, chairman of Senate Committee on Elections, which reported the bill favorably in that body; Representatives A.G. Shoup and W.T. Burns, who, among others, ably supported the bill in the House; W. W. Shorthill, secretary to the governor.
(Courtesy of Frances E. Willard Memorial Library, Evanston, Illinois)

On January 10, 1917, James Wickersham, Alaska's delegate to Congress, along with Dan Sutherland, a member of the Territorial Senate of Alaska, and Cornelia Hatcher, president of the WCTU in Alaska, testified in favor of prohibition before the House of Representatives' Committee on the Territories and for control over the Alaska Fund, 25 percent of which supported education. Mrs. Hatcher stated that before coming to Washington, D.C., the trio had assured the teachers that "we could count upon Congress allowing us to at least administer our own funds. It is our money; it is not anybody else's money."[28] Six days later Mrs. Hatcher joined three representatives of the national WCTU to provide similar testimony before a Senate committee. In this appeal, Mrs. Hatcher emphatically requested that Congress "either release to us the Alaska fund, to be disbursed under Territorial authority, or supplement it by an increased appropriation for schools."[29] The pleadings were favorably received, and on March 3, 1917, Congress provided for the emergency by passing a new act that allowed the Alaska legislature to appropriate territorial funds for educational purposes. This led the Alaska legislature to prompt enactment of the Uniform School Act of 1917, which, among other things, stipulated that funds for the support of schools were to come from municipal and territorial sources.[30] Margaret confidently reported to the *Union Signal*:

Cornelia Templeton Hatcher and Margaret Keenan.
(Courtesy of Frances E. Willard Memorial Library, Evanston, Illinois)

All the schools outside of incorporated towns are to be provided for entirely from the territorial treasury. The schools in the incorporated towns will receive seventy-five percent of the necessary funds from the territory and twenty-five percent from direct taxation in these towns. For the first time in the history of Alaska the education of the boys and girls of the territory will be carried on with clean, untainted money.[31]

When Margaret arrived in Fairbanks in the summer of 1916, in addition to prohibition and funding for education, Fairbanks was abuzz with talk about the construction of a railroad, begun in 1915, from Seward to Fairbanks that, according to Margaret, indicated progress but would end the frontier era. She and others heralded the positive impact the railroad would have by lowering prices and shortening travel time to the Outside, but at the same time they lamented the negative impact this tie with the world would have. One concern was that Fairbanksans would have to use dimes, nickels, and pennies, heretofore considered only souvenir coins and playthings for the children, instead of gold as currency. Margaret enjoyed telling the story about a young schoolboy who was given two nickels by a gentleman from Outside. After inspecting the coins front and back, the youngster tossed them into a nearby cuspidor. His action caused Margaret to remark, "They represented no value to him. That day is passing and with it some of the old-time methods, also some of the old-time extravagance."[32] On another occasion she watched two small children sitting on the boardwalk playing with coins. When she asked them what they were doing, they demonstrated their game and explained that the winner kept the coins. The coins were silver dollars! Margaret knew that such luxury was short-lived, and these examples convinced her that Fairbanks children needed to learn different values. She also realized that with the coming of a railroad, the days of stagecoach and dogsled travel were limited.

Before dogs lost their importance in Alaska transportation, Margaret wanted to experience travel by dogsled. During her Christmas vacation in 1916 she hired a musher to take her down the seventy-seven-mile Fairbanks–Nenana Trail, where she spent a week at the new government railroad town as the guest of Renee and Thomas Riggs. He was the construction supervisor for the Interior Division of the Railroad Commission, and would later serve as Alaska's territorial governor from 1918 to 1921. The lifeless cold stillness of the gray twilight on a midwinter day filled Margaret with what she believed was the real spirit of winter, and by journey's end she felt pride in her 150-mile accomplishment. Someday, she believed, when she was a "real sourdough," she could say, "Why yes, I was down that right-of-way long before the railroad was built."[33]

In addition to savoring the natural beauty that she had trouble finding words to describe, Margaret acquired a respect for the people who had lived for so long in this remote area removed even from the conveniences that Fairbanks offered. She later mused, "I do so envy these sourdoughs their something, I do not know exactly what it is; something that has been acquired by years of straight think-ing and hard hitting in this land so fresh from the hand of God."[34] It would be another eight years before Margaret would have an opportunity to again explore the North's wilderness.

In April 1917, at the request of President Woodrow Wilson, Congress declared war on Germany, and American soldiers were soon sent to Europe to assist the Allies. The American public was slow to accept their involvement, but by fall most expressed a growing commitment to the war effort, and people gave their money and time and voluntarily limited their consumption of vital commodities. Although many of Margaret's friends Outside assumed that Fairbanks was too isolated to feel the effects of the war effort, she did not hesitate to recount the same sincere public cooperation in Alaska as in the rest of the country.

In the fall Alaska's First Lady, Annie Hall Strong, invited the women of the Interior to join with the ladies of the "Coast" to raise six hundred dollars, the amount necessary to purchase and maintain a bed at the American Ambulance Hospital near Paris. Fairbanks women immediately accepted the challenge and established a Ways and Means Committee to determine the methodology to achieve the goal. The ideas of a food sale and benefit ball were approved, "then came an uneasy pause," Margaret remembered.[35] "This was essentially a woman's project; it must be especially successful; it would be if only it were advertised in some unique way; why not a woman's edition of the daily paper?"[36] At the urg-ing of his wife, Nell, W. F. Thompson, editor of the *Fairbanks Daily News-Miner*, reluctantly offered his staff and equipment for the project with the understanding that half of the gross receipts from the sale of the paper would go to the women and half to the newspaper. His other stipulation was that Margaret Keenan must be the editor.

At the end of September Margaret secured commitments from fifty-three women to contribute articles, and for the next two months she spent every evening after school at the *News-Miner* office organizing, editing, and arranging. While Margaret concerned herself with the actual copy, Katherine Pratt sold advertising, and Harriett Hess organized the assembly and sales of the paper. Mrs. Pratt's unorthodox method of selling advertising space brought in record amounts of cash. Margaret commented:

> I never could learn what their rates were; in fact, I do not think they had any. They just sized up their victim with an appraising eye and charged all the traffic would stand. They not only could induce a man to turn his pockets inside out, but they could make him feel that he was honored by being asked to do so.[37]

After two months' work, Margaret and her committee were ready to produce their Women's Edition of the *Fairbanks Daily News-Miner* on Thanksgiving Day. The night before, an outraged Thompson appeared at Margaret's desk for the first time since the project began. He expounded that the paper could not yet go to press because it did not include a "news" section by his journalistic definition. Emphatically Margaret explained that letters home from Fairbanks servicemen abroad constituted news, and furthermore, the press must roll in order to free the women in the circulation department in time to prepare their Thanksgiving dinners. Finally Thompson conceded that as the editor Margaret could make the decisions. The paper, containing war, news, and editorial sections, was printed, the ladies had time to prepare dinner, and the Women's Edition appeared for sale as promised on November 29.[38]

When the final receipts were tallied, the Fairbanks women smugly announced that "a community of less than fifteen hundred people calmly jingled out of its pockets the price of six hospital beds in one month, at the same time meeting all of their demands of the hour."[39] Five Canadian-born residents of Fairbanks pledged six hundred dollars among themselves—the total hoped for by the entire Alaska Territory! When Thompson received his half of the proceeds, he acknowledged that he had actually profited by $87.50. Needless to say, this fact pleased Margaret, as did the general goodwill that resulted from this effort. After the paper appeared, she received only two calls from upset contributors: one demanding an explanation for why her initials were omitted from a two-inch piece, another complaining that her middle name was misspelled in the byline of a feature article on the front page.[40] Margaret excused these women's outbursts because both were "cheechakos," or newcomers to the North.

In another effort to demonstrate that Alaska was not too far removed from the United States to be concerned about the war, Margaret joined in the national appeal to sell Liberty Bonds to replenish the government's defense coffers. This fund-raising campaign was directed at the Fairbanks schoolchildren and, like the

Liberty Bonds were sold during World War I to help replenish the national treasury. Margaret initiated the program in Fairbanks schools so that children could participate.
(Gaustad Bartlett Collections, UAF-1972-0156-00132, Archives, University of Alaska Fairbanks)

Women's Edition of the newspaper, netted phenomenal results. Each of the 186 students was expected to buy one bond over the next year. To kick off the effort, Margaret personally underwrote ten thousand dollars worth of bonds, no small commitment on her salary. "The public received the announcement with a gasp of astonishment, followed by a gleam of appreciation," Margaret proudly recounted.[41] Arrangements were made with the First National Bank to establish accounts for each student in grades one through twelve to facilitate the time purchase of the bonds paid for with money they had earned. "In some way it must represent sacrifice," Margaret instructed the student body.[42] A few hours after Margaret announced her plans to the assembled students, a girl approached her to make an outright purchase of one bond with fifty dollars she had earned from picking and selling berries the previous summer. While this transaction was handled, a line formed of other students ready to commit. That day Margaret sold fifteen bonds, some fully paid, some on time. Her scheme was off to a good start.

The plan allowed a student to pay one dollar down and two and a half dollars monthly, the bank holding the bond until the final installment was paid. "This was no mean contribution in bookkeeping from a bank that had formerly required a minimum of three hundred dollars to open an account, and had shoved back to the depositor all nickels and dimes as scrap metal."[43] To help the children earn their money, Margaret established an employment office in the school, which provided job opportunities for the students that could be carried out in conjunction with their Junior Red Cross requirements. Many of the girls worked at domestic chores and child care, while the boys eagerly seized the opportunity to cut ice from the Chena River and sell it to individual homes. Most Fairbanksans used water delivered by the water wagon at twenty-five cents for ten gallons, which was full of minerals and not suitable for fine laundry or shampoos. Therefore the boys' delivery of ice, which thawed into soft water, was an appreciated luxury.

By the end of the school year in 1918, the Fairbanks children had purchased 210 $50 bonds, an average per student of $60.84, for a grand total of $11,049.79.[44] The results of this nationwide school Liberty Bond sale were published in a leading education journal, and no other district equaled Fairbanks. In all, the people of the United States contributed over $21.5 billion through this campaign.

As previously mentioned, the Liberty Bond sale ran simultaneously with the students' Junior Red Cross activities. During Christmas week of 1917, with the temperature hovering around fifty-five to sixty below zero, the students conducted a local contribution drive netting $3,192.50 from 798 subscribers.[45] These funds gave Fairbanksans the satisfaction of knowing that they supported six French and Belgian war orphans for a year. As before, the entire community joined together in these fund-raising efforts. John Butrovitch, who later became an Alaska legislator, was seven years old at the time and remembered that Mrs. Arthur McGowan offered a cash prize donated to the French Orphan's Fund in the name of the young Fairbanksan who offered the best name for a stray cat that she had adopted. In the spirit of the cause, John submitted the name "Orphina" and won the contest, receiving cake and ice cream as his tangible reward.[46]

In July 1918, Margaret stopped in at the local Red Cross headquarters while visiting in Seattle. Certain that the Fairbanks contribution was inconsequential to the overall fund-raising efforts, Margaret felt insignificant. She reservedly introduced herself to an official who electrified her with his congratulatory handshake. Bewildered, Margaret asked exactly what Alaska had done to warrant such a greeting. Enthusiastically the Red Cross worker informed her that Alaska raised seven times its assigned contribution but then cautiously asked if she had seen the quota assessments sent from Red Cross headquarters. "Oh, yes," Margaret replied, "but no one ever paid much attention to them. It was taken for granted that we would exceed our quota, so no one gave them much thought."[47] As Margaret departed the Seattle Red Cross office with the knowledge that Alaska had more than contributed its share, she hoped that this kind of attention would convince people Outside that the territory should be taken seriously.

In the summer of 1916, while visiting friends in Seattle before moving to the Interior, Margaret was given a letter of introduction to Martin Luther Harrais of Chena, the neighboring gold camp to Fairbanks. When her boat docked at this camp seven miles downriver from Fairbanks, she inquired after Harrais but

learned that he was out at his mine. Because of Martin's prominence as a successful miner, businessman, and civic leader, it was impossible for Margaret to forget
him. However, it was not until the spring of 1917, when he moved into a room
across the hall from her at the hotel/rooming house where she was staying, that
she actually met him. Not long afterward he confided in her that he thought her
a "damned fine girl."[48]

As they became acquainted, Margaret fell in love with this man with a foreign
accent who had been born in Riga, Latvia, Russia, on January 2, 1865. Under the
German occupation of northern Latvia, Martin's parents became slaves of the
Germans. Years later, in a letter to the United States Civil Service Commission
requesting the opportunity to serve in the United States military during World
War I, Martin explained that when he was fourteen years old an act of disre-
spect toward the Germans had resulted in his expulsion from Russia, and he was
shipped to sea. For nine years his life followed the tide until, at age twenty-three,
he came ashore at San Pedro, California, eager for the American experience. He
had learned some English while sailing on British ships but realized quickly that
his vocabulary was mostly profanity. The need to improve his language encouraged him to place the small Russian Bible that had belonged to his mother next
to a King James version and pick out corresponding words, thus improving the
quality of the language of his new home. With night courses and classes at a local
YMCA, Martin received an education while working in the Southern California
shipyards. When the shipbuilding industry in California declined, Martin moved
to Seattle. With enough education to consider college, Martin entered the University of Washington in 1892 as a subfreshman and received a B.S. degree in mining engineering with academic and athletic honors five years later. The day after
graduation he and four other young men headed to the Dawson goldfields via
the Chilkoot Pass. When the Yukon gold waned, Martin moved over to Alaska's
Tanana Valley to continue his mining efforts. He profited financially and emotionally in Alaska's Interior, and when Margaret once asked him what it was about life
in the North that attracted and held men, he remarked:

> Outside we were all swimming around and round like goldfish in a glass bowl; but
> some of us thought we would like to try being a real fish in a real stream. Alaska
> gives us just that—a chance to be a real fish in a real stream. After that we do not
> like to go back to the glass bowl again.[49]

His quest for a larger freedom matched Margaret's, although she had not yet
made a commitment to remain in Alaska, and mounting frustration at work
caused her to rethink her future there.

A supply order for school year 1917–18 had been mailed Outside with specific
shipping instructions. Margaret was outraged when a letter arrived from the
supplier advising that to save money they had selected a less expensive shipping

method. The alternate route was slower, and the school's supplies for the year spent the winter frozen in somewhere on the Upper Yukon. Incidents like this, coupled with an unusually cold winter and disappointment at not being selected for the Territorial Board of Education, left Margaret at year's end feeling dissatisfied. Even praise from the school board did not improve Margaret's outlook. "You have modernized our 'bone dry' curriculum by the introduction of domestic science and manual training and have thereby taught our boys and girls the dignity of labor as well as given them the highest ideals for their future manhood and womanhood."[50] In spite of adulation and adequate funding, without hesitation Margaret accepted a position as principal of schools in Shenandoah, Iowa, where her brother Thomas, former vice president and mathematics professor at Western Normal College, was now practicing law. Margaret did not record Martin's reaction to the news of her planned departure. However, she did mention that he was suffering financial losses and did not invite her to stay on with him. When she left Fairbanks, Martin traveled with her on the Fairbanks–Valdez stage down the Richardson Trail as far as Chitina, where he got off to go to work for the Kennecott Copper Corporation as head of a reconnaissance party in the Upper Chitina district. A few months later Margaret could still recall that moment of parting.

> The muscles of my throat tighten yet as I think of that last hour in Chitina—the attempt at casualness, the enforced cheerfulness by which we each tried to make the situation a bit easier for the other. We faced stark loneliness for an indefinite period, but there was no alternative. Even love in a cottage presupposes a cottage.[51]

Margaret arrived Outside in the midst of the devastating 1918 influenza epidemic and became critically ill. While sick she contracted pneumonia and nearly died. In favor of convalescing, she tendered her resignation to the Iowa school district and settled in San Diego, where she bought a small house with a large yard. In addition to gardening, Margaret involved herself with the California WCTU and served as publicity woman for the national WCTU. When Martin received word of the seriousness of her illness, he realized the depth of his feelings and joined her in California. Margaret and Martin were married at the San Diego YWCA on October 25, 1920. A few years previously she had commented to a friend that if she did marry Martin, it would only happen when she also made up her mind "to marry Alaska, too."[52] At the age of forty-eight she apparently felt comfortable with a commitment to another marriage and to life in the North.

The newlyweds spent the winter of 1920–21 in California, and the following summer Martin returned to Alaska to continue his mining. The next several years were spent in this manner: "delightful winters together in California and lonely, tho fruitful, summers separated."[53] By 1924, Margaret had regained her strength and desire to return to Alaska, and she forestalled Martin's trip south that fall by accepting a teaching position at McCarthy. Realizing that home is where the heart

Margaret at the San Diego, California, home where she lived
during her recuperation from influenza, ca. 1918.
(Harrais Family Papers, Box 8, Folder 128, Archives, University of Alaska Fairbanks)

is, she packed and headed back to Alaska. If she had any doubts about her decision, they were dispelled on the journey north, during which, she recalled, "everyone visited with everyone else; cabin boy and captain, passenger and flunkey, all mingled together in the common-democracy-of-the-North. With swift realization I said to myself, 'These are my people. After an enforced absence of several years, I am going home.'"[54]

In McCarthy, Martin continued his mining interest while Margaret settled into their three-room log cabin. She gave glowing reports of the living room, but the kitchen proved most comfortable, and she remarked later that "for the first time in my life I am content to sit alone at a table long enough to eat my meals. Ordinarily I am up roaming around with my food in my hands, shifting from straight chair to rocker and back again, trying to read a magazine, anything to dispel the loneliness."[55]

For the next eight years Margaret taught school at McCarthy, instilling in the children the principles of temperance and thrift as she had in Skagway and Fairbanks. Summers were spent with Martin at his mining claim enjoying the search for copper and hiking and horseback riding into the nearby mountains and canyons. While at McCarthy, Margaret witnessed with pride the first female jurors performing their duty and continued her involvement with the WCTU, accepting the position of president of Alaska's chapter. In the late 1920s a national move commenced for an amendment to prohibition, and Margaret was offered a leadership position in the newly formed Women's National Commission for Law Enforcement and Law Observance—an organization that represented fifteen million women nationwide. Because acceptance required a move to the East Coast, Margaret declined the invitation, stating that it "was out of the question since there was no place for The Skipper in that scheme of life."[56] Her commitments to Martin and Alaska were beyond negotiation.

Martin (left) and Margaret at the Harrais camp, Upper Chitina region near McCarthy.
(Harrais Family Papers, Box 8, Folder 125, Archives, University of Alaska Fairbanks)

Martin outside the Harrais homestead at Chitina.
(Harrais Family Papers, UAF-1971-0080-00003N, Archives, University of Alaska Fairbanks)

McCarthy schoolchildren. Margaret is standing at lower left, wearing a light-colored hat.
(Harrais Family Papers, Box 8, Folder 125, Archives, University of Alaska Fairbanks)

In 1932, the Harraises felt the impact of the Great Depression when they lost all of their savings in a failed Seattle bank, and their hope that Margaret's salary would suffice was shattered when, due to decreased enrollment, the McCarthy school closed. The final blow came a few years later when the railroad closed into Martin's mining claims, eliminating access. Destitute, the Harraises moved to Cordova, where Martin planned to take over the operation of a rundown sawmill. Margaret recalled that "youth was gone, enthusiasm was gone; all that remained was one another and a grim determination to keep our chins above water and be self-sustaining."[57] A summer at the mill proved that the business was not salvageable, and just when they wondered what next to do Margaret was offered a contract to teach at Ellamar, a small coastal village between Valdez and Cordova. The new job was not of the caliber to which she had become accustomed, but now that she was married more prestigious opportunities were closed to her. Not in a position to quibble, Margaret accepted the teaching job, leaving Martin in Valdez, where he subsequently received a political appointment as U.S. commissioner and bought and renovated a six-room house. Margaret left Ellamar at the close of the 1935 school year to rejoin Martin and enjoy life in the first house they had ever owned. She bragged to friends in the States that the house had a bathroom and instructed that such luxury could not be taken for granted: "It costs over three hundred dollars to install one, and eternal vigilance to keep it from freezing up in winter."[58] After three years alone in a one-room log cabin at Ellamar, Margaret enjoyed the conveniences of oil for heating and cooking, a vacuum cleaner, an electric clothes washer, and an electric pump on the well.

Margaret and Martin.
(Harrais Family Papers, UAF-1971-0080-00003, Archives, University of Alaska Fairbanks)

The summer of 1935 Martin headed to Mineral Creek, still hoping to find a copper mine. In his absence, Margaret stepped in as commissioner, and later, try- ing to explain that her duties included all of the functions of a county courthouse, she recalled several cases handled on her first day. A commercial fisherman, whom she knew, was brought before her charged with drunkenness. Margaret sentenced him to ten days in jail, the length of time until the fishing season opened, with a promise that as soon as he was freed he would go right to sea and not get drunk.

He replied, "No, I no promise. I might happen to get drunk again, and I no like to double-cross you."[59] In another case, a man pled innocent to charges that he stole a boat, stating that he had just taken it. He was sentenced to six months in jail "in which to contemplate the difference [between] stealing and just taking."[60] On another occasion Margaret attempted to make a civil marriage ceremony as impressive as possible. She nearly lost her composure, however, when the "ardent groom, instead of the demure 'I do,' responded, 'Bet your life; hope to die!'"[61] The knowledge and experience gained that summer became important to Margaret in the future.

At summer's end Martin returned from his mining work with news that he had found a promising mining property. To earn the necessary money to purchase and develop the claim, Margaret agreed to return to teaching at Ellamar for one more year. When she came home to Valdez for Thanksgiving she found Martin busily planning for the next season's work. Therefore, a few weeks later when back at Ellamar, she was shocked to get word that Martin was critically ill. When Margaret got to Valdez she learned that he was hospitalized in Seward, but stormy weather prevented her from making the trip by seaplane to be at his bedside. While she waited for the weather to improve, news came that Martin had died of cancer at five p.m. on Christmas Day. He was buried in the Pioneer Plot of the Seward cemetery.[62]

In keeping with her frontier philosophy that no one is interested in how things are done back home or overindulgence with personal problems, she grieved privately and busied herself as commissioner, receiving an official appointment to the position immediately after Martin's death. She was grateful for the previous summer's experience in the job. In addition she organized a mining library of more than three hundred Geological Survey Bulletins and nine cases of maps of Alaska. She renewed her interest in gardening, advocating the use of greenhouses, and maintained an active role in the community. Margaret was chairperson of the Valdez Community Hospital Board, a member of the Territorial Board of Education, and active in the statehood movement. After statehood in 1959, Margaret was appointed deputy magistrate for the third judicial district, a position she held until 1962, when frail health forced her to retire.

Off and on during these years, Margaret made an effort to publish a manuscript of her remembrances of life in Alaska. At the suggestion of family and friends Outside who received her annual Christmas letters that summarized the year's activities and observations, Margaret compiled this collection for publication consideration. In the fall of 1932 she sent the first five chapters to her niece and namesake, who was then associated with the English department at the University of Michigan. The typed, single-spaced, four-page response was less than encouraging, and the analysis that the preliminary work was wordy and cluttered with lengthy sentences punctuated randomly by semicolons was to the

Commissioner Margaret Harrais (center) with Vide Bartlett (left) and Alaska's delegate to
Congress, E. L. (Bob) Bartlett (right).
(Harrais Family Papers, Box 8, Folder 127, Archives, University of Alaska Fairbanks)

point. As to content, Margaret's niece chided that her aunt's experiences were not
unique—they could be, and were, duplicated elsewhere. "Too many women now
are charting unknown seas and are making howling successes of their charts,"
she stated.[63] She further informed Margaret that she knew several women who
took for granted their prominent positions in the business world. Commenting on
the chapter that described the Fairbanks war effort, Margaret's niece adamantly
instructed that it should be deleted entirely because preoccupation with war and
patriotism only keep alive a spirit of hate. In her comments about the "emotional
significance" of the manuscript, her niece remarked, "I found the frequent hushed
reference to swearing…decidedly out of place in the annals of an Alaska pioneer."[64] Whether Margaret edited her work based on her niece's suggestions is
unknown, but from the copy that remained with her papers it would appear she
did not. She may have considered her niece's analysis evidence of a generation gap,
liberal thinking, or uninformed remarks from an individual who had not experienced Alaska and made clear "it is the sort of life I should not endure for long but
would welcome for a holiday."[65] A subsequent letter from the niece indicated she
may have reacted too harshly in her initial review of the manuscript, and as if to
seek forgiveness, she recommended Margaret contact the Writers' Workshop, Inc.,
a literary agency in New York City.

University of Pennsylvania history professor and Alaska historian Jeannette
Paddock Nichols offered more encouragement, which no doubt pleased Margaret,

when she commented, "Your subject matter is interesting, and is told in appropriate style.... You have the delightful style and the material for a best-seller, and I'll look for its appearance with keen anticipation."[66] Dr. Nichols even predicted that the royalties would be sufficient for Margaret to posthumously publish Martin's autobiography, which sat in manuscript form.

By 1943 Margaret was in contact with Anita Diamant, an agent for the Writers' Workshop, Inc. Although Diamant believed Margaret's material had the potential to become "a most compelling narrative," she negated the compliment by stating that "you haven't quite used it as effectively as you might."[67] She concluded her four-page criticism by refusing to act as agent.

Margaret, however, did not accept the refusal, and in another letter to the agent, defended her work. Diamant's second effort to quell Margaret was more specific. She explained that the flowery descriptions and Victorian style were unacceptable and her sentimentality cloying. Diamant's accusation that Margaret's prudishness suggested she wore collars up to her ears and dresses to the floor was the last straw. Margaret's final response was short and succinct.

> No, I shall not attempt to do anything with [the] manuscript along the lines you suggest.... I was writing the spirit of Alaska in an attempt to correct some of the damphoolish [sic] ideas you people have of us, but that seems to be hopeless. Evidently we are too far apart in our basic ideas to be of any assistance to one another.[68]

There is no evidence that Margaret continued efforts to find a publisher, even though Alaska's Senator Bob Bartlett proclaimed that if her letters were turned into book form, they "could rank in importance with the Diary of Judge Wickersham."[69] In 1946, Margaret's former Fairbanks pupil, Edby Davis, wrote to her that he thought her manuscript publishable, but too bad it had not been printed twenty years ago. "Now," Edby reminded her, "Mary Lee Davis & others has [sic] flooded the market with simular [sic] material."[70] But Margaret steadfastly defended her reason for creating the manuscript. In a letter to Dora Sweeney of Juneau she wrote, "I tried to interpret the real heart and soul [of] Alaska, instead of glorifying infamous characters."[71] Eventually, Margaret's unpublished manuscript, titled "Alaska Periscope," was placed in a three-ring binder and shelved in the Valdez Public Library.

Margaret's life was filled with dramatic events of her own making. Therefore it was no surprise that she chose her ninetieth birthday to mark her official retirement from civil service. Governor William A. Egan praised Margaret's contributions to education, the Democratic Party, and government service by awarding her Alaska's Certificate of Merit. Senator Bob Bartlett read into the Congressional Record that "she has possessed always a young spirit in a pioneer land [and] her life has been a model of all that is good and decent and constructive."[72] For fifty years Margaret was a leader who never let gender inhibit her role. In fact,

Margaret working at her desk, ca. 1960.
(Harrais Family Papers, UAF-1971-0080-00002, Archives, University of Alaska Fairbanks)

at the beginning of her professional career in Idaho she was told that the Nampa school district "never had a man Principal who did as thorough [and] constructive work."[73] Margaret established and perpetuated a reputation as a woman who was interested in developing well-balanced young men and women, and her commitment to high standards of excellence was lauded and emulated.

On March 27, 1964, the town of Valdez was evacuated as a result of the Good Friday earthquake, which devastated the Prince William Sound region of south-central Alaska. Margaret, who had been in failing health since the previous fall, was taken inland to Gakona Lodge, where a friend recalled she sat in the lobby knitting her 114th afghan.[74] After an asthma attack she was admitted to Faith

Hospital in Glennallen, where she died on April 26, a few months short of her ninety-second birthday. In keeping with her wish to be buried where she died, she was interred at the Glennallen cemetery. When her estate was settled, it was discovered that the now-mature U.S. Savings Bonds that Margaret had purchased during the past forty years still named the WCTU as beneficiary. Rather than cash these in 1932 when she and Martin lost their savings, Margaret at the age of sixty was willing to resume teaching to earn a living. Her final contribution to the temperance cause amounted to almost seventy thousand dollars.[75]

Margaret's devotion to temperance began as a child and guided her professional and personal life to selfless heights. It is therefore ironic that toward the end of her life, when praised for her societal contributions, no mention was made of her commitment to the WCTU or the influence the organization's philosophy had on how she lived her life or performed her service to her community.

5

Mary Lee Cadwell Davis
1884–1966

No one is indentured to live and labor here!
We have come and we remain solely
because we find in our Alaska "the makings"
for interesting, wholesome, and useful living.[1]

Mary Lee Davis

In 1914, Congress decided to fund construction of a railroad from Seward to Fairbanks. Assured of permanence, Alaskans celebrated, and commercially minded Fairbanks residents looked forward to the day when their mining camp would become a town. The Fairbanks Commercial Club proudly announced "there is every reason to suppose that Fairbanks will be as distinctively the metropolis of the Greater Alaska of the future as it has been for more than a decade the banner camp of the bottled-up territory."[2] In addition to believing that the lack of reliable year-round transportation had delayed the Interior's development, many residents were convinced that misconceptions about the climate and a belief that the inhabitants were "foolhardy miners hobnobbing with Eskimos in the Interior" stagnated migration to Alaska and retarded its population growth.[3] United States Geological Survey reports indicated immense mineral wealth still to be had if mining costs could be reduced, and this information, coupled with news of the railroad, piqued the interest of people Outside. If coal for fuel could be brought from the Nenana fields into Fairbanks to replace the dwindling timber supply, minerals that required mechanized extraction could be more economically mined.[4] The railroad was a harbinger of prosperous times and ensured Fairbanks's future.

The field was ripe for serious-minded writers to eradicate the image of the frozen northland, dancehall girls, and the wild stampede days popularized by novelists such as Rex Beach and Jack London. A realistic portrayal of Alaska's potential would surely convince Americans that the territory had been a wise purchase after all. For a young woman interested in mining and intent on launching a professional writing career Fairbanks presented unique opportunities, and Mary Lee Davis's arrival in the Interior during the summer of 1917 placed her in a unique position.

Related to colonial New Englanders and American pioneers, Mary Lee grew up on the Atlantic seaboard surrounded by history, culture, and educational and social opportunities. Born April 20, 1884, in Westfield, New Jersey, and named for her maternal grandmother, Mary Lee was the daughter of Newton Woodworth Cadwell, a lawyer turned Presbyterian minister, and Jane Worrall Criswell, the "golden-haired music teacher of Chapman Seminary" in Clinton, New York.[5]

A precocious child, Mary Lee later wrote that when young she "loved all sorts of mysteries and weird things, and weaving queer stories all alone."[6] Her father took his work very seriously and was frequently absent from the home or preoccupied with his responsibilities, while her mother fulfilled the expectations of a Victorian preacher's wife. Frequent entertaining, visiting the sick, and making calls left Jane "foolishly busy" in Mary Lee's opinion.[7] Her parents' obligations left Mary Lee alone with a bright and active mind, and she struggled to find her place. When her father was home, he spent much of his time in his study, and Mary Lee discovered that this book-lined room provided a retreat and time alone with him. After all, she thought, he might need help writing his sermon or her opinion on some other matter. This concerned Mrs. Cadwell, who did not share her husband's or daughter's love for philosophical discussions. To avoid disappointing her mother, when Mary Lee entered the study she always carried a juvenile book for appearance's sake in case Mrs. Cadwell appeared.

Reverend Cadwell enjoyed the obligations of his profession, but Mrs. Cadwell found her role more challenging. A self-described lighthearted person by nature, she found the life of a preacher's wife oppressive. Feeling inadequate and weak compared to her husband, Jane looked to her daughter for strength. In church meetings she insisted Mary Lee sit beside her so she could hold her hand. Needing Mary Lee as she did, she resented her daughter's time spent in the study, playing with other children, or weaving fairy tales, which she shared with confounded church members. In an attempt to please her mother, Mary Lee distanced herself from her playmates. Mary Lee found her mother peculiar, and an incident associated with learning her catechism heightened her awareness that there were confusing differences between herself and her mother, and between her parents themselves.

Mrs. Cadwell offered to oversee Mary Lee's memorization of the Presbyterian catechism. Partway through the process Reverend Cadwell challenged Mary Lee to a convivial recitation match to see who could get the farthest without looking at the text. Confidently Mary Lee began then suddenly stopped when she noticed her father's expression change from a smile to one of shock. Mary Lee indignantly defended her memory, sure she was correct in what she said, until she noticed the beleaguered look on her mother's face. Apologetically Mrs. Cadwell explained that she had given Mary Lee the catechism book that she herself had used as a child, not realizing that each presbytery has a different version. She assured her husband that she would hide her little "heretical book" and use his text. This episode left Mary Lee puzzled about theological matters and feeling that her parents did not realize the sincere effort she had put forth to learn. These thoughts deepened until she admitted that maybe the different way each parent perceived the catechism book more accurately represented differences between them and their relationship with each other.

Eventually, Mrs. Cadwell went "away, for a time, to rest," believing that "different air and rest" would put things right.[8] In her mother's absence, Mary Lee shouldered additional obligations in the church and in the home, which was indeed heavy for a young schoolgirl, but Mary Lee stoically accepted the challenge. Her mother's behavior caused Mary Lee to become more self-reliant as she took on more responsibility, and perhaps she learned not to trust others for her own happiness and direction in life. Like her father, she became independent and focused.

Through Mary Lee's child's eyes, Mrs. Cadwell was not easy to explain, but the women of the church considered her "the ideal minister's wife."[9] When Jane Cadwell died July 3, 1914, in Rome, Italy, while touring the continent with her husband following their son Paul's graduation from Oxford,[10] a friend of hers who considered her perfectly suited for her role and a good partner for the reverend said, "I cannot imagine Dr. Cadwell without her."[11] The women of Westfield and the Olivet Presbyterian Church in Atlantic City, New Jersey, where the Cadwells had moved in 1902, honored Jane's "Christian character" and friendship with a bronze plaque hung in the Atlantic City church. An article written about the memorial service, held October 11, 1915, indicated that Reverend Cadwell and Paul participated in the ceremonies; however, no mention is made about Mary Lee's attendance.[12]

Although she felt somewhat stifled and confused as a child, Mary Lee delighted in the unique opportunities provided by her ancestry and social connections. Her father's great-grandmother was related to John Quincy Adams, and her mother's grandmother, Agnes Herron, was a cousin of Nellie Herron, who married William Howard Taft.[13] These connections afforded periodic invitations to White House functions, and in March 1909 Mary Lee had the opportunity to "pour" at Mrs. Taft's first tea.[14] Revolutionary War pensioners on both parents' sides granted Mary Lee membership in the Daughters of the American Revolution (DAR), and in 1924, she was one of thirteen to charter the Alaska Chapter of the DAR founded in Fairbanks.[15] Another family connection provided Mary Lee firsthand knowledge of Alaska. S. Hall Young, the veteran Alaska Presbyterian missionary and adventurer, repeatedly traveled to the East Coast to solicit financial support for his mission work in southeast Alaska. A friend of Reverend Cadwell, Young visited the Cadwell home on several occasions, and Mary Lee later remembered herself as a "leggy silent child, sitting in [her] father's study and listening star-eyed to Dr. Young describing the wonders of Alaska and that trip with Muir."[16] Mary Lee was enthralled by Young's re-creation of his famous trip with naturalist John Muir to explore Glacier Bay, a region of extraordinary beauty and natural drama northwest of Juneau in southeastern Alaska, and she recorded that Young "was the first Alaskan I had ever seen, and all he told made pictures," images that later became reality.[17] These brief meetings inspired in Mary Lee a desire to capture for herself the beauty and stories of Alaska. Years later when she lived in Alaska, Mary Lee was honored to have Dr. Young visit her and her husband in their Fairbanks home.

After graduation from Lincoln High School in Westfield, New Jersey, Mary Lee entered Wellesley College in 1902, the expenses paid by wealthy friends of her parents.[18] At Wellesley Mary Lee found an environment that nurtured her love for philosophical discussions and reading, and instead of reproach for storytelling, the Scribbler's Club encouraged it. Samples of her prose and poetry appeared regularly in the *Wellesley Magazine*, the school's literary journal. Mary Lee excelled academically, and in her junior and senior years she received highest honors as a Durant scholar, was elected Phi Beta Kappa, and graduated with a B.A. degree in the spring of 1906. That fall Mary Lee entered Radcliffe College and earned a master's degree the following year. With such a remarkable academic career it would appear that Mary Lee found college to her liking. However, her 1928 alumnae information form indicated that she would "probably not" choose Radcliffe for her graduate work if she had to do it over again, and as if to emphasize her displeasure, she further noted that her brother Paul's choice of Harvard Law School had no connection to her selection of Radcliffe.[19] Her academic file gives no explanation for this remark; however, her comment that "nagging policy of the then college authorities" made the year "most uncomfortable" gives a clue to her resentment. Mary Lee's irritation that her major professor hesitated to return her thesis may also have left Mary Lee embittered.[20] A fuller explanation may lie in her answer to a question asking what she considered to be the value of her graduate work:

> As a woman who has lived for years on the frontier in mining camps & isolated towns, I consider a mind equipped with conveniences for doing its own thinking as a *sine quo un*. But I have observed that a college education does not invariably produce such a condition & that it can be arrived at, equally well, by other routes.[21]

Clearly, Mary Lee learned through her experiences that it takes more than a formal education to live a full and discerning life.

The same benefactor who paid for Mary Lee's education provided her a year in Europe after graduation. This opportunity should have created experiences and observations worth saving in story form; however, the only mention of this trip in her published work appeared disguised in an article about a later trip to Colorado. A family friend recalled that Mary Lee cut short the European adventure to return

Mary Lee graduated Phi Beta Kappa from
Wellesley College in 1906.
(Courtesy of Wellesley College Archives)

home in 1908 to marry John Allen Davis of Sioux City, Iowa, a 1907 graduate of
the Massachusetts Institute of Technology.[22] After their October 29 marriage, the
Davises established their home in Washington, D.C., where Allen, as he was known,
worked as a junior geologist with the United States Geological Survey (USGS).

In the spring of 1909, Mary Lee and her "Seven-eighths," as she affectionately
referred to Allen, made a trip to the American West. Like her father, who desired
a hard job on the untamed frontier, Mary Lee was captivated by the thought of
doing things for the first time in an unpopulated land far from the bustle of the
city. The Davises rode the Overland Limited on the Union Pacific Railroad into
Wyoming, where they picked up some scientific equipment that Allen was to
take into Colorado. Near the old Fort Bridger military reservation they met up
with a Mr. Miller, who provided them with horses and acted as their guide for
the four-day trip. Although Mary Lee had horseback-riding experience from her
childhood, selecting which horse would carry her into Colorado was a frightening
experience. Knowing she had to choose, she picked "a wiry, wee Indian pony ... as
the least of many evils."[23] When Mr. Miller instructed her not to pull on the bit
but turn him by the neck, Mary Lee remarked that riding a Western pony was
more like her experience riding a camel in the Sahara desert, a comparison that
puzzled Miller.

For several days the party wound its way along a well-defined trail southeast-
ward through Wyoming, the very northeast corner of Utah and down the Green
River into the valley of the Yampa. Craig, Colorado, their final destination, was the

quaint small town that Mary Lee imagined, and as the only metropolis for miles around, its post office, general store, and drugstore drew scattered frontiersmen. Mary Lee felt at home immediately and wondered, "Do you suppose it is some far-felt touch of our inheritance of pilgrim and pioneer that calls to us from this new West? Why is it, on this unbroken soil, that we are never homesick to hearken back to the harlot cities of the East?"[24] Although Mary Lee found her summer living in a tent on a mountaintop at the Colorado radium mine exciting, her western experiences do not figure significantly in her writing. Perhaps they paled by comparison to her years in Alaska. These experiences may have also proven that an East Coast girl could withstand the rigors of outdoor living, knowledge that Mary Lee may have needed in Alaska.

Mary Lee's frontier adventure continued when, after several years in Denver as a mining engineer with the U.S. Bureau of Mines, Allen received an assignment to create a mine experiment station for the federal Bureau of Mines in Fairbanks.[25] Wearing a large-brimmed hat that had become her trademark, Mary Lee, along with Allen and their purebred Airedale, Monte, arrived in Alaska's Interior on July 15, 1917.[26] In the midsummer's never-ending daylight, Mary Lee had the opportunity to study the surroundings as the steamer *Alaska* pushed its way up the Yukon River. Her first impressions of Fairbanks were of golden fields of ripening wheat and poles along the city streets. Although she had prepared herself for Alaska, she had to rethink her preconceptions. No, the land was not snow-covered year-round, and the government agricultural station suggested an up-and-coming industry. And those poles were not totems; they supported wires that took electricity into almost every home and carried telephone messages around town and out to the mining camps on the creeks.

Rental property was scarce, but Mary Lee and Allen found a rambling six-room cabin next to St. Matthew's Episcopal Church on Front Street facing the river. They paid forty dollars a month for rent. After arranging antique New England furniture, Mary Lee got acquainted with the features of her new home. A large wood-burning furnace in the basement sent heat up through vents in the floor, and the double-paned windows helped to keep the warmth inside. A well, sunk under the furnace so that it would never freeze, was equipped with an electric pump that pushed water into a holding tank in the attic that provided running water from spigots by gravity. The cabin boasted a large, well-equipped kitchen and one of only six modern bathrooms in Fairbanks. On cold winter days Mary Lee invited friends, who otherwise would have to go to one of the public bathhouses, to luxuriate in the large porcelain tub. After the bath she offered a nice cup of coffee and a convivial visit that enhanced the total experience.[27]

Two months after her arrival, Mary Lee learned about Margaret Keenan's Women's Edition of the *Fairbanks Daily News-Miner* and agreed to contribute an article. Most of the features included in this special edition of the newspaper, which

In 1909, Mary Lee and her husband, John Allen Davis, spent the summer at a mining camp in Colorado where Allen was on assignment as a junior geologist with the USGS.
(Courtesy of Wellesley College Archives)

was designed to raise funds to support a bed at the American Hospital in France, covered topics such as how women could help the war effort and why America was at war. Mary Lee, however, spun a sophisticated twist to a scientific article about how Alaska could help the United States win the war. She proclaimed that the soldiers needed more than clothes and food—they needed hardware and equipment made from metals. Therefore, she concluded, "mining is an essential industry for the winning of the war," and she reasoned that the country needed to increase its supply of primary resources such as "natural gas and oil, coal, iron and metalliferous ores."[28] Alaska, she claimed, was the logical location for this extraction, and thus she began more than a decade of writing about the northland in an effort to educate Americans about Alaska's wealth and potential.

Mary Lee and her purebred Airedale, Monte, outside her Fairbanks home.
(Robert and Jessie Bloom Papers, 63-89-01N, Archives, University of Alaska Fairbanks)

Mary Lee's books and articles, most of which were published after her departure from Alaska, reveal that she accepted the popular notion at the time that the federal government had grossly neglected Alaska's needs, and her opinions about natural resource development parroted reports by Alfred H. Brooks, USGS geologist for Alaska, and Sumner S. Smith, United States mine inspector. Like the professionals, Mary Lee wanted to see the coalfields opened for private leases, construction of the railroad between Seward and Fairbanks, oil exploration, and agricultural development. She also agreed with the far-sighted secretary of the interior, Walter Lowrie Fisher, who predicted that Alaska's scenic beauty would become "one of its greatest financial assets."[29] Promotion of Alaska became Mary Lee's preoccupation, and she lived her life to experience the greater landscape, develop close friendships, and participate in community affairs, all in an effort to better understand and appreciate her new home.

Alaska's people fascinated Mary Lee. As a newcomer to the Interior she was struck by their friendliness, feelings that were enhanced over time. She was in awe of the sourdough who had "sought the unblazed trails behind the grim dark hills," and the founders of Fairbanks who "had already sowed their untamed youthful oats in untamed youthful camps" and were ready to put down roots and create a permanent community.[30] Mary Lee listened carefully when a woman told her that "everyone has come to find something, or to forget something," and she enjoyed the fact that a community of independent-thinking nonconformists is never dull.[31] Whatever their reasons for choosing to live in Alaska, the Fairbanks population was a group of similar-minded people who, Mary Lee believed, were making history, and she intended to record the progression of events and emotions.

In particular, Mary Lee was interested in the other women who had chosen to make Alaska their home, and she was proud to join forces with them. More women than ever before were moving to Alaska as they accompanied their husbands north, spurred by the 1893 economic depression in the United States. Word of unbelievable gold strikes was all it took for many to make the decision to move north. According to historians Claire Rudolf Murphy and Jane Haigh, unlike women who pioneered the American West and dealt with disease and Indian attacks, those who came north were threatened "by the brutal cold, rugged territory, and vast unpeopled distances."[32] Mary Lee reveled in writing about these experiences. But most of all, she believed that "we women need that vision of ourselves as vital agents in this world of great events."[33] Although she encouraged progress, she warned that being different was not inherently wrong and careful thought must be part of any judgment of others. Her book *We Are Alaskans* profiles some of the people who Mary Lee believed were helping to reshape the image of Alaska without abandoning their individuality and cultural roots. Featured were Fannie Quigley, the self-sufficient miner of the Kantishna region; Tillie Paul, the Tlingit Presbyterian missionary from southeastern Alaska; Janet Aitken, the dog-mushing prospector at Arvada; S. Hall Young, the exploring Presbyterian minister and Mary Lee's lifelong friend; and W.F. Thompson, the bold and forthright editor of the *Fairbanks Daily News-Miner*, who had a reputation for expressing his daring opinions "with no round-about or weasel words."[34] Misconceptions about the North and what kinds of people chose to make it home and why were connecting themes threaded throughout her writing.

Mary Lee attributed distance from Alaska as the primary reason for misunderstanding, and she readily chastised easterners who "get positively irritated when we write to you of flowers and gardens. You want to hear of igloos and mukluks and Polar bears.... You want to hear about the cold, always.... You want to hear of dissimilars."[35] She responded to such demands by elaborating on how much mineral wealth had been shipped from Alaska since the turn of the century, the summer's light and warmth, agricultural development, and the cultural and technological similarities with the Outside. Although she urged people not to come seeking their fortune in gold, she did offer a litany of reasons to seek a northern adventure:

A thirst for the far-away, the old human land-hunger, the desire to be masterless, the wish to escape the crowding economic complex, a will set against regimentation, sheer and clear daredevilty, a youthful love of new experience and adventure ... and more.[36]

Her advice to queries from women considering a move north was succinct: "No woman should come to Alaska who has a narrow-gauge or single-track mind. It is a broad country, in more than one meaning."[37] She also cautioned that "pioneer women are all workers, and the woman who works is independent—it is the woman who has forgotten how to work who has lost her freedom."[38] In general, however, Mary Lee extended a welcome invitation to "cast in your lot and covenant with this new colony of your race overseas, claim here your ten square miles of masterless space, and learn for yourself far the best answer to that question 'Who lives in Alaska—and why?'"[39]

Mary Lee identified a corollary between the treatment of New England colonists and Alaska pioneers. She set out to influence policy making in Washington, D.C., by writing about what she perceived to be unfair treatment and government neglect of the territory. Writing primarily for an eastern audience, she ignored any connection between the American western frontier and Alaska pioneering. Instead she developed a theme comparing the experiences of Alaskans with the misunderstandings that New Englanders first suffered. The colonials, she professed, were cast as religious fanatics, convicts, and general misfits fearfully huddled together in a savage, Indian-infested land, while Alaskans were portrayed as derelicts hiding out in this distant frozen country overrun by Eskimos, a parallel that she believed blue-blood easterners would understand. Her assessment of life on the new frontier was that Alaskans were "just other latter-day New Englanders, doing a similar hard pioneering job with much the same faith in themselves and for their chosen land."[40] Clearly Mary Lee's experiences provided the raw material for her later writing, and after her arrival in Fairbanks she wasted no time getting involved in the activities shaping the territory.

Although raised Presbyterian, Mary Lee joined St. Matthew's Episcopal Church because of her husband's faith. Her friend Jessie Bloom remembered how Mary Lee commented on "her Presbyterian knees which she found so difficult to bend at the proper time."[41] The Episcopalians founded St. Matthew's Church and Hospital in 1904, and opened the first library in Fairbanks. In addition to holding a seat on the library's board of directors, Mary Lee was a member of the church Women's Guild that operated a public reading room, opened in 1906 to provide books, magazines, and newspapers to local residents, the outlying mining camps, and the jail. In their history of St. Matthew's Church, Arnold Griese and Ed Bigelow recorded, "there was little a miner in Fairbanks could do on long dark winter nights if he did not drink or did not frequent saloons. Worst of all there was little reading matter in the new gold camp."[42] Appeals to church members Outside resulted in a flood of periodicals, all sorted by volunteers in the church rectory. When donations outgrew available space, the work was moved to the Pioneer Hotel, where the proprietor asked only that the hotel lobby be well supplied with magazines in exchange for the accommodations. By 1908 more than twenty-five thousand pieces of reading material arrived annually, and in 1909 George C. Thomas, secretary of the Episcopal Mission Board, donated the money to build a library that would replace the reading room. Bishop Hudson Stuck's donation of one thousand books augmented the growing supply of periodicals and filled the George C. Thomas Memorial Library when it was dedicated August 5, 1909, shortly after the death of its namesake.[43]

Mary Lee's regular donation of periodicals to the reading room helped supply the Fairbanks community with reading material. An avid art and music enthusiast, she subscribed to forty-seven journals on the subjects. After reading each issue she cut out articles of particular interest and added them to scrapbooks that she had maintained since childhood. In her effort to share the cultural arts with Fairbanksans she frequently gave talks to groups based on her scrapbooks, and she generously shared her collections with individuals who expressed interest in learning more. When she had finished reading her magazines, she donated them to the library's reading room, and her friend Meta Bloom Buttnick remembers that this act of kindness could lead to frustration for subsequent readers. On one occasion a gentleman got interested in a particular article only to find the page on which it continued cut out and undoubtedly pasted into Mary Lee's scrapbook. In anger he "threw the magazine across the room."[44] Mary Lee's dedication to the library inspired its growth and undoubtedly helped launch it into what it is today.

Mary Lee's affiliation with the Episcopalians also provided a literary outlet. The Fairbanks diocese published a quarterly magazine designed to keep church members Outside informed about the Alaska mission. This forum gave Mary Lee the opportunity to share her progressive philosophy about the territory, and the February 1919 edition carried her article expounding on Alaska's wealth and contributions to the United States in hopes of convincing readers that development of the North's natural resources "would enable Alaska, the stepchild of the nation, to...do what the opening of the West did after our Civil War—pay the Nation's War Debt!"[45]

Previous experience as an Associated Press reporter prepared Mary Lee to handle the local Red Cross chapter's publicity, and periodic articles written for the *Fairbanks Daily News-Miner* fostered a professional relationship with W. F. Thompson, the newspaper's editor. A contribution printed in September 1918 provided knitting instructions for socks and sweaters to clothe American servicemen in France, and another article that fall called the women of Fairbanks together to sew 250 garments for French refugees. The invitation to gather at the library the following Wednesday and Saturday for sewing marathons was followed by emphatic instructions to every woman to organize her schedule with these dates in mind. Mary Lee's rhetorical plea that "you will do this, won't you, oh you patriotic women of Fairbanks?" left no question in anyone's mind about participation.[46] The American Red Cross established a chapter in Fairbanks in 1917, and the organization continues to provide life-saving services in Alaska. In 1964, after the devastating Good Friday earthquake in southcentral Alaska, Governor William

St. Matthew's Episcopal Church operated the first library, or reading room, in Fairbanks. They
provided this service until 1942 when local government assumed the responsibility. Mary Lee
served on the reading room's board of directors and donated magazines.
(Courtesy of Candace Waugaman)

A. Egan designated the Red Cross as the state's official relief agency to provide
emergency services to Alaskans in times of disaster.

Although she considered the *News-Miner*'s Thompson more of a colleague than
a friend, Mary Lee liked him and respected his candid approach to journalism.
However, the Fairbanks flu epidemic in the spring of 1920 caused some tension
between the two. Thompson had a "survival of the fittest" attitude and showed
little empathy for the weak. Believing as he did that Fairbanks was the land for a
strong chosen few, he did not accept the seriousness of this epidemic, which had
hundreds of residents hospitalized or sick in their own beds. After all, there was
no place for weakness in "Our Town," as he referred daily to Fairbanks in his column about the goings-on in the community. "These rotten and annoying rumors"
that the flu had invaded Fairbanks did not "contribute anything of moment to the
camp's progress," Thompson stated in early April in a short article tucked on a
back page entitled, "Is No Flu in Our Town."[47] By the twenty-sixth of the month,
however, Thompson admitted that "Fairbanks has the flu, and it is growing day
by day," and his editorial for the day was devoted to home treatment procedures.[48]
The crises peaked a couple of days later, and by April 28 the *News-Miner* proudly
announced, "EVERYTHING IS ALL RIGHT: FAIRBANKS TOO HEALTHY FOR IT."

Mary Lee wrote an article that was published in the August 1929 issue of the
Atlantic Monthly, and later became a chapter in her book *We Are Alaskans*, that
described the flu epidemic and her role as a volunteer night-duty nurse in the

makeshift hospital in the basement of Immaculate Conception Catholic Church. She did not hesitate to report hundreds of deliriously ill patients, an overflowing hospital, and insufficient numbers of trained medical personnel to meet the demand. Red Cross volunteers provided what care they could. No doubt Mary Lee was saddened when she heard of incidents such as Mrs. Gus Bostrom, who was delivered of a stillborn son as she lay dying from influenza.[49]

Another case, however, provided some comic relief. In her report, Mary Lee explained how one doctor pronounced a patient dead only to find him revived, having suffered an asthma attack. This incident and the doctor's eventual permanent departure from Fairbanks on the first boat out that summer were never mentioned by Thompson, the journalist who could report only the best about Fairbanks.[50] In fact, Mary Lee later learned that in Thompson's effort to keep the entire epidemic a secret from the rest of the world, he never mailed copies of the "flu-time papers" to out-of-town subscribers. Breakup came and with the outgoing rotted ice went the disease that had disabled Fairbanks. By late June the seriousness of the episode was only a memory, recollection of which was restored vaguely by a *News-Miner* advertisement announcing a Fourth of July "Patriotic Ball" at which "tickets for the May Day dance which was canceled because of the flu will be honored."[51]

In addition to telling of community activities, Mary Lee derived great pleasure in describing the houses in which she lived, not to brag but rather so that people Outside would know of Fairbanks's luxury. After renting a log cabin for two years, the Davises had the opportunity to buy a house on Cowles Street at the corner of Fifth Avenue. This large eight-room home boasted a lawn with planted birch trees, an open fireplace, hot-water heat, polished oak floors, a vacuum system, cellar ash chute, large screened porch, double garage, and superior insulation. In fact, it was a house within a house with a six-inch space between the two walls filled with sawdust to retain the warmth in winter and repel the heat of the summer.[52] After several winters in the house, Mary Lee remarked to a friend that her father used twenty-five tons of coal to heat his similar-sized house in Atlantic City, while she and Allen used nine. Filled with family heirlooms, the Davis house was considered one of the most elegant homes in town. It was added to the National Register of Historic Places in 1972.[53] Today, the "Mary Lee Davis House," as it is called, has undergone major renovation and is described in the brochure for self-guided walking tours of Fairbanks distributed by the Fairbanks Convention and Visitors Bureau. In the spring of 2008, it opened as the Alaska Heritage House Bed and Breakfast.

Travel around the territory also provided subject matter for Mary Lee's writing. In 1916, United States mine inspector Sumner S. Smith announced the establishment of a Fairbanks mining experimental station to help prospectors determine the value and quantity of minerals, which in turn was expected to help them decide whether or not to launch full-scale mining operations.[54] As chief

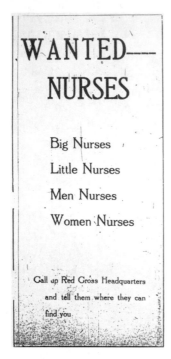

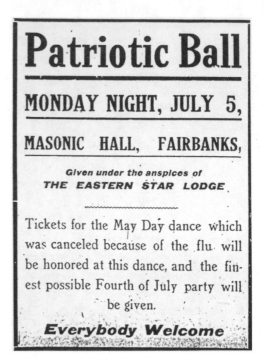

LEFT: An advertisement ran in the *Fairbanks Daily News-Miner*
for volunteer help during the 1920 influenza epidemic.
(Fairbanks Daily News-Miner, May 7, 1920)

RIGHT: This notice for the Fourth of July Patriotic Ball ran in the
Fairbanks Daily News-Miner.
(Fairbanks Daily News-Miner, June 28, 1920)

mining engineer for this station, Mary Lee's husband, Allen, was required to travel the territory to make assessments, and an adventurous Mary Lee accompanied him. The summers of 1918 and 1924 were spent canvassing the Seward Peninsula, and one August, almost too late in the season for such an adventure, she and Allen journeyed six days by dogsled and packhorse into the Kantishna region. They traveled the route that is now the Denali Park road into Wonder Lake and up Moose Creek to Joe and Fannie Quigley's homestead. For eleven days Joe and Allen scouted the region for mineral prospects while the women tramped the hills and Mary Lee reveled in Fannie's life story. Even though Fannie praised her for being the first woman to come into this country through the "new passes," Mary Lee considered the time with Fannie "one of the rarest treats [she had] ever known and worth a dozen pioneering high-pass trails."[55] Her adventures continued, and like many Alaskans who wanted one last look at the wilderness before the railroad "messed it up," Mary Lee and Allen walked the Broad Pass section of the trackless rail bed halfway between Anchorage and Fairbanks. An unexpected spring bliz-

Mary Lee outside her Cowles Street home. Her home is now operated as a bed and breakfast. *(Robert and Jessie Bloom Papers, 63-89-02N, Archives, University of Alaska Fairbanks)*

zard hit with a vengeance, and they were "caught crawling along like flies upon the mountain slope."[56] It took them nearly two weeks to traverse the one hundred miles. Mary Lee recorded that friends in Fairbanks became so worried when they did not arrive home on time that W. F. Thompson wrote what amounted to an obituary for the couple, who, he declared, were lost on their crazy, foolhardy adventure. Not long after, Mary Lee traveled the same country in a Pullman observation coach. As the train crossed Broad Pass, Mary Lee

> looked far down [and] recognized from this now conquered height that very chasm of our three-fold avalanche, where we had struggled for three days imprisoned in the

mountains' heart, walled with impenetrable snows, against archaic night. This was the conquest men had dreamed, this was the bourne of all those lonely trails.... Again mere Man had answered the insuperable challenge, with his dream-spun steel.[57]

In the 1920s, travel books and articles about Alaska were plentiful. According to the *Boston Herald*, too many of these "have been written on second hand information or as a result of a hasty summer visit."[58] When Mary Lee began to publish her works about Alaska, she gained immediate credibility because she had actually lived in the territory, seen the landscape she described, and knew the people about whom she wrote. In an effort to present Alaska in an appealing way to the general public, writers like Frank G. Carpenter, who created a series of more than twenty books chronicling his globe-trotting observations, sublimated cultural differences and romanticized nature. When Carpenter wrote that he could provide his readers "a close view of Mount McKinley only from hearsay and from the magnificent pictures of Belmore Browne, the noted mountain climber of the Camp Fire Club of America," Mary Lee countered with a personal and insightful introduction to a chapter about this majestic mountain and its surrounding country that she explored on foot with her husband.[59] To emphasize her firsthand experience, she bragged that "ever since we first came to Alaska I had been looking out from my south window...over toward that great mountain hung upon the clouds—Denali, Last-Home-of-the-Sun."[60] When Carpenter attempted to ease his readers' fear of wildlife by stating that "Alaskan bears, caught as cubs, make wonderfully tame pets," Mary Lee described her "most intimate—and, I'll confess, a much too intimate!—contact with grizzlies" in a five-page description of following and being followed by a sow with two cubs on a trek into the Kantishna country.[61] She concluded her account by forthrightly admitting that she did not "recall this episode with any great pride, for I was scared and there's no use denying it. But—my only regret is, I do wish I knew just how big that grizzly was!"[62]

Her knowledge of and friendships with Alaska Natives placed Mary Lee's work far above that of most Alaska travel writers. Her friendship with Muk-pi, an Inupiaq Eskimo woman from Nome who died in the 1918 Seward Peninsula diphtheria epidemic, convinced Mary Lee that Alaska Natives "are human beings, not mere quaint curiosities."[63] Although she was very familiar with Outside efforts to reshape the lives of these early inhabitants of the North, she argued that it was a great mistake to feel sorry for them and an even greater one "if we try to change their ways too much toward our ways."[64] While the popular literature presented reassuring assessments that the Natives had become Americanized in their dress, religion, types of houses, and even their use of United States currency, Mary Lee repeatedly stressed the importance of learning about and understanding their values and customs, and warned against assuming an attitude of cultural arrogance. Reflecting upon what she saw as "a superabundant measure of that rare gift of the gods—free, constant, bubbling laughter that neither fear nor night nor winter stillness when the Sea is closed, can still in them," eased Mary Lee's pain when her friend Muk-pi died in the summer of 1918.[65]

By September 1924, the Alaska Agricultural College and School of Mines was sufficiently developed to assume responsibility for the work previously conducted by the mining experimental station, and Allen Davis was reassigned to Washington, D.C. The Davises sold their fully furnished house on Cowles Street to the newly formed Fairbanks Exploration Company for $2,050.[66] When Mary Lee and Allen left Alaska in October 1924, Mary Lee left behind her antique furniture, crystal, and silver, but took with her notebooks full of rich memories. Oddly, she never recorded how she felt about leaving; however, a newspaper article that documented their departure stated the Davises were "loath to depart."[67] Back on the East Coast, Mary Lee wrote four books in quick succession that recounted her experiences and observations about her seven years in the North. Perhaps this was Mary Lee's way of expressing and sharing her emotions.

All of Mary Lee's books about Alaska were published by the W. A. Wilde Company of Boston, whose marketing strategies resulted in enormous success. Her first book, *Uncle Sam's Attic*, appeared in 1930, followed closely by *Alaska: The Great Bear's Cub*, a children's book that came out later the same year. Of the former, Dan Sutherland, Alaska's delegate to Congress, remarked, "Mrs. Davis has produced a master piece," and enthusiastic book critic William Lyon Phelps "placed it third on his list of best books of 1930."[68] The book was later published in Braille by the Library of Congress.[69] However, the recognition and acclaim given *Uncle Sam's Attic* by East Coast reviewers was not necessarily shared by Alaskans. In his October 1930 editorial in the *Alaskan Churchman*, Reverend Michael J. Kippenbrock praised Mary Lee for her "delightful insight into the history and present status of the Last Frontier," but he criticized her nearsighted assumption that Fairbanks represented the whole of Alaska:

> The viewpoint is that of one who has lived in Fairbanks, and it is the Interior that is suggested to be the true Alaska. We feel that it is hardly fair for those who have crossed the high mountain ranges and descended into valleys of the Yukon and the Tanana to claim a superiority over those Alaskans who have pioneered other sections of this great empire-to-be.[70]

Thirty years later Melvin B. Ricks, author of *A Basic Bibliography of Alaskan Literature*, remarked that Mary Lee's writing style "may be buoyant and fanciful in one chapter and painfully detailed, slow-moving, and repetitious in the next."[71] Ricks further remarked on the inaccuracy of many of her statistical and historical facts, which she apparently did not check, and he questioned that living in Alaska for seven years qualified anyone as an "'old, old resident'" as Mary Lee claimed for credibility. Nevertheless, *Uncle Sam's Attic* made a significant impact.

When *Alaska: The Great Bear's Cub* appeared in print a few months later, it filled the void for credible Alaska literature for young people. Replete with pen-and-ink drawings by famed Alaska naturalist Olaus Murie, this charming volume informed its readers how glaciers are born, why the author of *The Night Before Christmas* should have taken another look at reindeer hooves, how totem poles are made and what they represent, how the Russians "discovered" Alaska, and more. By 1931, these two books had brought Mary Lee enough attention that she was a frequent lecturer about Alaska in the Washington, D.C., area. Her notoriety brought in more than seven hundred letters from interested readers.[72] Admirers suggested that Mary Lee write a third book about her Alaska experiences that presented sketches of individuals without a focus on Alaska's potential economic value to the United States. She took heed, and in 1931 the W. A. Wilde Company published *We Are Alaskans*—described as "gossipy, warm, intimate tales" about the Natives and the Anglos who call Alaska home.[73] A Washington, D.C., newspaper called it "a book of people, of customs embodied in sturdy characters," and the *Boston Herald* praised Mary Lee's effort by agreeing with her that "yes, indeed, people are more interesting than places."[74]

Mary Lee's fourth, and least well-known volume, about the North is a novel set in the Klondike gold-rush era, which tells the story of a "Yukon adventurer" as he floated the Yukon River. The promotional literature that accompanied this 1933 publication suggested that *Sourdough Gold: The Log of a Yukon Adventure* "is a man's story, the fruit of that high courage which finds its deepest tap-root in the secret, silent place."[75] The publisher suggested that the book expressed "a frankness and an insight won from a long abiding within the hidden North."[76] However, the story made it clear that the sourdough hero spent only one year in the Klondike. If Mary Lee could be accused of exaggerating her seven-year stay in Fairbanks into lengthy residency, the Yukon River float hero hardly qualified as a sourdough. Nevertheless, for want of firsthand material about Alaska, *Sourdough Gold* received minor attention.

As Mary Lee wrote her books, many of the chapters appeared individually in such leading literary magazines as *Scribner's* and the *Atlantic Monthly*. In 1929, she published two interviews with women who then resided in the White House in *Ladies' Home Journal* and *Good Housekeeping*, but the 1933 appearance of *Sourdough Gold* marked the end of Mary Lee's professional writing career.[77]

The Davises continued to live in Washington, D.C., where Allen ultimately held the position of chief engineer for the information division of the Bureau of Mines. While Meta Bloom Buttnick visited the Davises in the mid-1930s, she read portions of an autobiography that Mary Lee had drafted and hoped to publish. However, there is no record of this accomplishment, and the manuscript cannot be located.[78] When her father died in 1936, Mary Lee became custodian of his personal recollections written in short-story form. Reverend Cadwell had frequently talked about publishing these "little adventures…as an ideal of physical & moral courage to young men," and there was discussion of Mary Lee taking on the task. By 1950 this had not happened and Paul, Mary Lee's brother, suggested that Hamilton College, their father's alma mater, might be interested in pursuing the idea.[79] The job was beyond Mary Lee's physical capabilities, and Hamilton College did not accept the challenge.

In the late 1930s, at the age of fifty-eight, Mary Lee had been struck by lightning, which left her visually impaired. In a letter to the *Wellesley Alumnae Magazine* in 1949 she wrote: "For over ten years I have been forced to conserve very carefully all close eye work, not to strain unduly the remaining good eye. So great Zeus himself wrote finis to my writing, in no uncertain terms. Even letters get short shrift."[80] Several years later, Allen's health deteriorated from the strain of two wartime government jobs, and he was forced to retire. The Davises moved from Washington, D.C., to Nantucket Island, Massachusetts, where they lived in Allen's family home, which he had inherited when his mother died in 1930. There, according to Mary Lee, they enjoyed the "gracious 18th century pace" and led "a very peaceful, almost monastic life."[81] In 1960, poor health and dwindling finances forced the childless couple to give up their home and move into the Nantucket Cottage Hospital, where Allen died on August 30, 1962. Three and a half years later, on January 25, 1966, Mary Lee passed away at the age of eighty-one. Her life and career were heralded in a lengthy obituary in the Nantucket newspaper.[82]

In writing about Alaska, Mary Lee's goal had always been to influence the federal government in its decision making about the territory, and her book *Uncle Sam's Attic* was her masterpiece toward this endeavor. Shortly after its publication two prominent industrialists, Robert E. Wood of Sears Roebuck and Henry Bradford Endicott of Endicott Johnson Corp. in Massachusetts, recognized the significance of what Mary Lee said. Allegedly they distributed copies of the book to each congressman and senator in Washington, resulting in a congressional delegation's visit to Alaska the following summer. Beginning July 13, 1931, the *Fairbanks Daily News-Miner* prepared the community for the entourage, and once their journey commenced, daily notices kept residents apprised of their guests' progress. While traveling north from Anchorage the group took a trip through McKinley Park (now called Denali National Park), and the *News-Miner* reported that even "MT. M'KINLEY [*sic*] SHOWS UP FOR CONGRESSMEN."[83] Clouds hung heavy over the park, obscuring the magnificent mountain that Mary Lee had hiked and written about. The *News-Miner* reported, however, that "suddenly the clouds just seemed to lift and float away and there was the mountain in all its marvelous grandeur. For over eighteen hours we all had a splendid view of Mt. McKinley, then the curtain dropped."[84] An editorial on July 28 welcomed the dozen or so distinguished visitors and announced a banquet in their honor that evening at the Model Cafe. When the politicians left Fairbanks the morning of July 30, the newspaper

Sourdough
Gold

THE LOG OF A YUKON

ADVENTURE

MARY LEE DAVIS

Brochure advertising Mary Lee's fourth book about Alaska, *Sourdough Gold*.
(Courtesy of Candace Waugaman)

proudly editorialized: "THEY CAME HERE AS STRANGERS THEY LEFT AS FRIENDS."[85] In thanking Fairbanksans for their hospitality, the congressmen pledged that "their friendship would be expressed in measures designed to aid the development of the Territory."[86] All this was a direct result of Mary Lee's first book.

When Mary Lee arrived in Fairbanks in 1917, Alaska's economy was depressed due in part to the absence of many men who had left to join the military during World War I. The federally funded Alaska Railroad, completed in 1923, which provided year-round transportation, raised hopes that the territory would attract Outside interest in development and thereby receive an economic boost. However, large-scale industrial and agricultural growth did not materialize. Many Alaskans, including Mary Lee, blamed Washington for this lack of expansion. However, Alaska historically has been short of capital for economic development, and therefore the state's abundant natural resources have always been developed by Outside investors.

In her subsequent and extensive writings about Alaska, Mary Lee shared truths about the people and what it was really like to live in the North, thereby debunking many myths. An opportunist who capitalized on her good fortune to live in Alaska during the territorial period, she affected thought in Washington, D.C., with her observations, which most likely influenced the decision for statehood three decades later.

Conclusion

[Alaska's pioneer women] were beautiful and likewise
possessed of every feminine charm as well as ability and pluck.
Many not only shared in the great work of developing mines
and conquering the frontier—but did the women's part
in founding here a land of permanence, rearing families and
establishing homes—making Alaska a homeland, which is the first
great essential in building an enduring state.[1]

THE JOURNALIST DAVID RICHARDSON wrote, "One of the fascinations of the gold rush era is that so many unlikely men (not to mention some pretty unlikely women) took part in it."[2] Also, there is a commonly held perception that women's lives in early Fairbanks were filled with drudgery and hardship. As we explore some of these "unlikely women," a theme emerges that makes their presence on the early Alaska frontier more plausible than improbable, and their lives appear far more genteel than assumed. A close examination of their lives reveals a pattern in which we can see these women, who came from varied backgrounds and circumstances, as geographically separated from other women of their time, yet very much within the broad scope of women's world.

First we see them moving north with little reservation, intent on improving their individual circumstances. Ellen Gibson and Margaret Keenan Harrais had previously established homes in the West for reasons of economic and professional advancement; therefore, their migration north was simply an extension of their beliefs that the frontier held opportunity and prospects for betterment. Although Jessie Bloom came to Alaska as an American immigrant, her buoyant attitude about beginning married life on a foreign frontier suggests an eagerness to do something unique and participate in the making of events. Aline Baskerville Bradley Beegler, also foreign born, seemed to sense that she could tread new paths to great heights in the North. Likewise, Mary Lee Davis, who had spent time in Colorado, found that Fairbanks fed her adventuresome spirit and provided fertile ground that enhanced her professional writing career. Armed with education, experience, and, as Margaret Keenan Harrais said, "a few extra drops of pioneering blood," their commitment to succeed in their chosen ventures enabled women to use their minds and hands first to establish homes and then to create a climate that nurtured individual and community growth.[3]

Most of the women who came to Fairbanks during its early years left behind comfortable homes in established communities. Historian Sandra Myres wrote that on the nineteenth-century American frontier "progress and economic betterment required sacrifice."[4] If Fairbanks women felt this, they did not speak of it in such blatant terms. Like women on the western frontier who believed the "wilderness could be conquered and civilization reestablished," Fairbanks women perceived adjustment to new conditions as what made them special and Alaska unique.[5] As such, they recorded with pride how they not only adapted to a harsh climate but thrived in it, and reverting to somewhat primitive conditions provided convivial challenges rather than setbacks. For instance, Ellen Gibson turned the lack of housing into a successful business venture for herself by building cabins to rent, and Jessie Bloom found using a woodstove for heating and cooking an exciting adventure. Women found that ordering food annually—which might seem like a hardship—in fact reduced the amount of time spent shopping, thus creating openings for other pursuits. Although Mary Lee Davis found life in Alaska more primitive than her East Coast upbringing, she capitalized on it by telling correspondents and readers of her published writings that life in the North was cosmopolitan and not significantly different from Outside. Most important, she raised the consciousness of Outsiders about Alaska's wealth and potential.

Months of overland travel from America's East Coast to the western frontier allowed women in the West to acquire new skills on the trail. This practical experience was useful to women as they settled into their new homes. Myres noted that "more important, the lessons of flexibility and adaptability learned under the conditions of trail life helped women to cope with new conditions and new problems."[6] Early Fairbanks women did not have the advantage of a lengthy journey to prepare them for frontier living. Their trip was not as arduous, but as previously noted, the earliest arrivals like Ellen Gibson were seasoned pioneers from Dawson, and subsequent residents like Margaret Keenan Harrais and Mary Lee Davis had lived in the West before moving north. Regardless of their experiences, early Fairbanks women had an eagerness for adventure that allowed them to remain flexible and tolerant and to adapt readily to their new conditions.

Except for the earliest arrivals, Fairbanksans did not have to contend with the construction of houses at journey's end like early newcomers on the western frontier, who arrived to empty land with only what they could carry. Housekeeping in the rural West "required a good deal of ingenuity" compared to that in Fairbanks.[7] Because cookstoves, washtubs and wringers, and similar household equipment were too big and heavy to carry overland, western women often cooked on open fires and improvised their laundry aids. Many Fairbanks women were able to bring in such household goods on the boats, but, if not, because Fairbanks was a supply center for outlying mining operations, many services and goods that added comfort and ease to day-to-day chores were available to purchase.

Historians have documented the isolation and resultant loneliness experienced on the rural American frontier.[8] By contrast, in choosing to live in a community, early Fairbanks women had companionship and organizations with which to affiliate. Women's church, social, and civic groups were formed early, and frequent dances and celebrations provided entertainment for most residents. In addition, school-related activities captured the interest of many. In Fairbanks, as in the West, teachers and youth leaders were prominent figures in the community.[9] Thus Margaret Keenan Harrais, the superintendent of schools, Aline Baskerville Bradley Beegler, a physician, and Jessie Bloom, who founded a private kindergarten and the Girl Scouts in Fairbanks, all enjoyed community respect.

As in the West, once homes, schools, and churches were established, Fairbanks women turned their organizational skills to creating a cultural atmosphere.[10] Music, drama, and literary groups developed along with political reform movements. Myres recorded that "although the women's rights movement started in the East, it was on the frontiers that the first significant gains were made."[11] For women like Jessie Bloom and Margaret Keenan Harrais, who had been involved previously with enfranchisement and temperance issues, Fairbanks allowed them to work actively within the structure of women's suffrage and the WCTU to effect political change simultaneously with women Outside.[12]

Due to national twentieth-century technological advances, Fairbanks quickly established a modern infrastructure that made it commensurate with, if not somewhat better than, other communities its size. Telegraphic and telephonic apparatus sped communications within the territory and linked Alaska with the Outside, and the availability of electricity allowed the use of irons and vacuum cleaners that lightened household chores. Rivers for transportation provided more mobility than was experienced in the early American West, and Fairbanks women like Ellen Gibson, Jessie Bloom, and Aline Beegler regularly journeyed Outside for business, medical care, cultural enhancement, and a milder climate. In Jessie's case, she outgrew her romanticized idea of the frontier, and the ability to spend extended periods of time outside of Alaska sustained her.

The American frontier and Alaska offered challenges to women's skills and provided opportunities to broaden the scope of their home and community activities, but economic opportunities were not significantly different from those in the East.[13] Women's entry into the business community, like Ellen Gibson's home laundry and rental cabins, provided needed services to a fledgling town, and Fairbanks's isolation from Outside resulted in more cooperation than competition. As on the American frontier, Fairbanks women generally found their niche in endeavors that were typically filled by women, like Margaret Keenan Harrais's position as superintendent of schools, and Mary Lee Davis's role as a professional writer.[14] Fairbanks women like Ellen Gibson could borrow money for their business ventures, and many women enjoyed successful careers, but as in the West, the Alaska women were not revolutionary in their choices. Nonetheless, women were proud of their accomplishments. Because men's attitudes generally paralleled those of women, and Fairbanks harbored an egalitarian spirit, women were encouraged and reinforced in their endeavors, and the community welcomed their contributions.

Women who arrived in Fairbanks prior to 1923 were eager participants in the growth and development of a community that was founded by seasoned pioneers. Organized government established an infrastructure that easily accommodated twentieth-century technology, and reliable river transportation provided necessary goods and leisurely travel into Alaska's Interior. Fairbanks became a comfortable place to live more quickly than did the American West, and Alaska attracted women who were eager to reestablish civilization as they had known it elsewhere. Women did not come to Fairbanks to escape what was going on Outside—they came to create an extension of the Outside in Alaska. They derived personal satisfaction from their efforts and felt intense pride for their contributions, which they knew had an impact on the development and permanence of Fairbanks.

After learning details of women's lives in early Fairbanks, I have concluded that for most of them their day-to-day existence was less complicated than my routine many years later at a rural Alaska cabin. There I do not have the advantage of a commercial laundry, water and firewood delivery, or stores within a short distance from which to make purchases. When I reach my destination, I have what I have packed and transported by river boat or snowmachine. If something is forgotten, flexibility and adaptation are the solution. If laundry is done, it is a "heat the water and slosh the clothes in a bucket" job; water is pumped from a well by hand and hauled on a sled; and firewood is located in the forest, cut, hauled to the cabin by boat or snowmachine, split, and stacked. The advantage that I have, however, is that I am not trying to civilize the wilderness. I go to the cabin to enjoy isolation and solitude and to live a less structured lifestyle for a time. When the need for conveniences and socialization arises, as it ultimately does, I can return rejuvenated to Fairbanks with all of its comforts and fit back into society. But, my idea of life in the wilderness is similar to environmentalist Bill McKibben's view of nature—"a certain set of human ideas about the world and our place in it."[15] Therefore, my time spent at a cabin in the woods is more a mind-set than a way of life.

My experiences in no way diminish the awe I feel for the women who dared to come to the almost-unheard-of community of Fairbanks, Alaska, in the early 1900s, where they created lives for themselves and influenced the quality of life for other pioneers. Alaska provided the stage on which they successfully acted out their idea of society. We today are all better off as a result of their courage, talent, and enthusiasm.

Appendix A

Analysis by Region of Foreign-Born "Pioneer Women of Alaska"[1]

Total foreign born: (66 individuals) = 31.57%

Region	Countries	Numbers of Individuals	Percentage of Total	Percentage of Foreign Born
Western European	Germany, England, Scotland, Wales, Ireland, France, Austria, Belgium	35	16.74	53.03
Eastern European	Latvia	1	Less than 1	1.51
Scandinavian	Sweden, Norway, Finland	16	7.65	24.24
Southern European	Italy	1	Less than 1	1.51
Canadian		13	6.22	19.69

---

1 Member's Recollections, RFP.

Appendix B

Analysis by Country of Foreign-Born "Pioneer Women of Alaska"[1]

Country	Numbers of Individuals
Germany	13
Canada	13
England, Scotland, Wales	10
Sweden	10
Ireland	7
Norway	5
France	3
Latvia	1
Austria	1
Belgium	1
Finland	1
Italy	1

1 Member's Recollections, RFP.

Appendix C

Analysis by Region of American-Born "Pioneer Women of Alaska"[1]

Total American born: (143 individuals) = 68.42 percent

Region	State/Territory	Numbers of Individuals	Percentage of Total	Percentage of American Born
New England	Maine, New Hampshire, Vermont, Massachusetts, Connecticut, Rhode Island	4	1.91	2.79
Mid-Atlantic	New Jersey, West Virginia, Maryland, Pennsylvania, New York, Delaware	14	6.69	9.79
South	Texas, Louisiana, Mississippi, Arkansas, Tennessee, Alabama, Georgia, South Carolina, North Carolina, Virginia, Florida	2	Less than 1	1.39
Midwest	Ohio, Indiana, Kentucky, Michigan, Illinois	28	13.39	19.58
Plains	North Dakota, South Dakota, Minnesota, Wisconsin, Iowa, Nebraska, Kansas, Missouri	42	20.09	29.37
West	New Mexico, Arizona, California, Nevada, Utah, Colorado, Wyoming, Montana, Idaho, Washington, Oregon	51	24.40	35.66
	Hawaii and Washington, D.C.	2	Less than 1	1.39

---

1 Member's Recollections, RFP.

Appendix D

Analysis by State of American-Born "Pioneer Women of Alaska"[1]

State/Territory	Numbers of Individuals
Washington	17
California	14
Pennsylvania	11
Michigan	10
Iowa	9
Minnesota	9
Nebraska	9
Illinois	8
Ohio	7
Oregon	7
Montana	6
Wisconsin	5
Colorado	5
Missouri	4
Kansas	4
Kentucky	3
South Dakota	2
New York	2
Connecticut	2
Tennessee	2
Nevada	2
West Virginia	1
Massachusetts	1
New Hampshire	1
Hawaii and Washington, D.C.	2

1 Member's Recollections, RFP.

Notes

Preface

1. Stephen Haycox, *Alaska: An American Colony* (Seattle: University of Washington Press, 2002), x.
2. Ibid., xv.
3. Ibid., 159–69.

Introduction

1. Agnes Thomas, Member's Recollections, Pioneer Women of Alaska, Rust Family Papers (hereafter RFP), Archives, Alaska and Polar Regions Department, Elmer E. Rasmuson Library, University of Alaska Fairbanks, no box number.
2. For extensive study of the founding of Fairbanks, see James Wickersham, *Old Yukon: Tales, Trails, and Trials* (Washington, D.C.: Washington Law Book Co., 1938; edited edition published by University of Alaska Press, 2009); Cecil Francis Robe, "The Penetration of an Alaskan Frontier: The Tanana Valley and Fairbanks" (PhD diss., Yale University, 1943); Terrence Cole, *E. T. Barnette: The Strange Story of the Man Who Founded Fairbanks* (Anchorage: Alaska Northwest Publishing Company, 1981); Dermot Cole, *Fairbanks: A Gold Rush Town That Beat the Odds* (Seattle: Epicenter Press, 1999).
3. Robe, 11.
4. Ibid., 115.
5. Ibid.
6. Ibid., 137–56.
7. For information about women's lives in early Fairbanks, see Margaret E. Murie, *Two in the Far North* (New York: Alfred A. Knopf, 1962); Jo Anne Wold, *This Old House: The Story of Clara Rust, Alaska Pioneer* (Anchorage: Alaska Northwest Publishing Company, 1976); Claire Rudolf Murphy and Jane G. Haigh, *Gold Rush Women* (Anchorage: Alaska Northwest Books, 1997).
8. Ellen Gibson to Tom, Elmer, and Joe Gibson, May 26, 1903, Sarah Ellen Gibson Collection (hereafter SEGC), Archives, Alaska and Polar Regions Department, Elmer E. Rasmuson Library, University of Alaska, Box 1, Folder 71.
9. Robe, 170–71.
10. Richard C. Wade, *The Urban Frontier: The Rise of Western Cities, 1790–1830* (Cambridge, MA: Harvard University Press, 1959), 28.
11. For photographs of the interiors of Fairbanks homes before 1910, see the MacKay and the Whitely collections, Archives, Alaska and Polar Regions Department, Elmer E. Rasmuson Library, University of Alaska Fairbanks.
12. D. Cole, 28.

13. Town Council Meeting Minutes, December 8, 1903, City of Fairbanks Historical Records (hereafter CFHR), Archives, Alaska and Polar Regions Department, Elmer E. Rasmuson Library, University of Alaska Fairbanks, Box 17.

14. "The Tanana Gold Fields," *Fairbanks News*, Special Number, May 1904, Candace Waugaman Personal Collection, 6.

15. Ibid., 9; Robe, 196–98.

16. Town Council Meeting Minutes, June 7 and 16, 1904, CFHR, Box 17.

17. Fairbanks Chamber of Commerce, *Tanana Valley Alaska* (Seattle: Metropolitan Press Printing Co., n.d.), Candace Waugaman Personal Collection.

18. Town Council Meeting Minutes, August 23 and September 13, 1904, CFHR, Box 17.

19. Robe, 11.

20. *Tanana Directory, 1907*, n.p., n.d., Archives, Alaska and Polar Regions Department, Elmer E. Rasmuson Library, University of Alaska Fairbanks, 116.

21. Stella Muckenthaller, "The Inception and Early Development Years of St. Joseph Hospital, Fairbanks, Alaska" (master's thesis, Catholic University of America, 1967), Alaska Nurses Association Collection, Archives, Alaska and Polar Regions Department, Elmer E. Rasmuson Library, University of Alaska Fairbanks, Series 7, Box 18, Folder 274, 44.

22. Alden M. Rollins, compiler, *Census Alaska: Numbers of Inhabitants, 1792–1970* (Anchorage: University of Alaska Anchorage Library, 1978), 574.

23. Isaiah Bowman, *The Pioneer Fringe* (New York: American Geographical Society, 1931), 27.

24. Ibid.

25. Jessie Bloom, "Watching Alaska Grow: The Personal Recollections of a Pioneer," American Jewish Archives Collection (hereafter AJAC), Archives, Alaska and Polar Regions Department, Elmer E. Rasmuson Library, University of Alaska Fairbanks, Box 4, Folder 43, 48.

26. James H. Ducker, *Carmack's Alaskans: A Census Study of Alaskans in 1900* (Alaska Historical Commission, 1983), 1, 5, 25.

27. Wade, 68.

28. An analysis of the membership data for the Pioneer Women of Alaska appears in Appendices A–D of this work.

29. Ida Crook, Member's Recollections, Pioneer Women of Alaska, RFP.

30. Wold, 181.

31. Margaret Brandt, Rae Boas Carter, Marshia Latimer Lavery, Genevieve Boas Parker, Anna Shiek, Member's Recollections, Pioneer Women of Alaska, RFP.

32. Wold, 182.

33. Ibid., 179.

34. *Tanana Directory, 1907*, 117.

35. "Don't Forget the Fair" and "Hospital Fair on Tomorrow," *Fairbanks Daily News-Miner*, October 14 and November 8, 1910.

36. "Reading Room Statistics," *Alaskan Churchman*, February 1907, 4.

37. Arnold Griese and Ed Bigelow, *O Ye Frost and Cold: The History of St. Matthew's Church, Fairbanks, Alaska* (Fairbanks: St. Matthew's Episcopal Church, 1980), 24.

38. "How Alaskans Backed Uncle Sam," *Alaskan Churchman*, February 1919, 56–60.

39. Town Council Meeting Minutes, September 11, 1917, CFHR, Box 19.

40. Governor J. F. A. Strong to Aline Bradley, February 7 and September 1, 1917; January 9, 1918, J. F. A. Strong Papers, Archives, Alaska and Polar Regions Department, Elmer E. Rasmuson Library, University of Alaska Fairbanks, Box 1, Folder 25.
41. Anna Penketh Caskey, Member's Recollections, Pioneer Women of Alaska, RFP.
42. "Choral Club Will Be Formed This Winter," *Fairbanks Daily News-Miner*, November 15, 1910.
43. Wold, 27–28.
44. Bloom, "1974 Memoir," AJAC, Box 3, Folders 36, 86.
45. Elliott West, "Beyond Baby Doe: Child Rearing on the Mining Frontier," in *The Women's West*, ed. Susan Armitage and Elizabeth Jameson (Norman: University of Oklahoma Press, 1987), 182.
46. Bowman, 27.
47. Bloom, "1974 Memoir," AJAC, 89.
48. Wold, 30.
49. Philip Knowlton, "What Fairbanks Was Like Way Back When," *Sunset*, July 1916, reprinted in *Fairbanks Daily News-Miner*, 23rd Annual Progress Edition, 1973, B-21, Skinner Vertical File Collection, Archives, Alaska and Polar Regions Department, Elmer E. Rasmuson Library, University of Alaska Fairbanks, File number 651.
50. Town Council Meeting Minutes, October 18, 1904, CFHR, Box 17.
51. John A. Clark, "Social Events," John A. Clark Papers, Archives, Alaska and Polar Regions Department, Elmer E. Rasmuson Library, University of Alaska Fairbanks, Box 1, Folder 37.
52. Ibid.
53. Murie, 38.
54. House, Conditions in Alaska, Hearings, House of Representatives, 1912 (Washington, D.C.: Government Printing Office, 1912), 162.
55. Ibid.
56. Clark, "Social Events."
57. "You Need Not Worry About That Divorce," *Fairbanks Daily News-Miner*, April 4, 1914.
58. Ibid.
59. Wold, 214.
60. Ibid., 183.
61. "Fairbanks, the Metropolis of Interior Alaska," *Pathfinder of Alaska*, May 1921, 17.
62. Stacia Rickert, Member's Recollections, Pioneer Women of Alaska, RFP.
63. Mary Miller, Member's Recollections, Pioneer Women of Alaska, RFP.
64. Catherine McCarthy, Member's Recollections, Pioneer Women of Alaska, RFP.
65. Mary Kline Bunnell, Member's Recollections, Pioneer Women of Alaska, RFP.
66. Agnes Thomas, Member's Recollections, Pioneer Women of Alaska, RFP.

Chapter 1

1. Ellen Gibson to Joe, Elmer, and Tom Gibson, May 8, 1903, SEGC, Box 1, Folder 69.
2. Frances Backhouse, *Women of the Klondike* (Vancouver/Toronto: Whitecap Books, 1995), 3.
3. Melanie J. Mayer, *Klondike Women: True Tales of the 1897–1898 Gold Rush* (Athens, OH: Swallow Press/Ohio University Press, 1989), 3.

4. Ibid., 19.
5. Backhouse, 3.
6. Joe Gibson to Ellen Gibson, August 26, 1897, SEGC, Box 1, Folder 11.
7. Ibid., September 29, 1897, Box 1, Folder 12.
8. Ibid.
9. Pierre Berton, *The Klondike Fever* (New York: Alfred A. Knopf, 1958), 174.
10. Ibid., 186.
11. Joe Gibson to Ellen Gibson, January 30, 1898, SEGC, Box 1, Folder 14.
12. Joe Gibson to Ellen Gibson, n.d., SEGC, Box 1, Folder 15.
13. Ellen and Joe were married September 28, 1881, in Brussels, Ontario (Audrey Loftus, "Lady Stampeder," *Alaska Magazine*, November 1977, 38).
14. Backhouse, 81.
15. Ibid., 78–79.
16. "Application for Grant for Placer Mining," Dawson City Museum and Historical Society, Dawson City, Yukon Territory, Canada; "Grant for Placer Mining," Certificate No. 20500, SEGC, Box 5, Folder 423.
17. "Sale Agreement," December 13, 1899, SEGC, Box 6, Folder 430.
18. Audrey Loftus, "Tom Gibson—Meat Hunter," *Alaska Sportsman*, June 1967, 19.
19. Elmer Gibson to Ellen Gibson, August 20, 1901, SEGC, Box 1, Folder 40.
20. Elmer Gibson to Ellen Gibson,, n.d., SEGC, Box 1, Folder 41.
21. Niece to Ellen Gibson, October 27, 1902, SEGC, Box 1, Folder 57.
22. M. L. Murphy to Ellen Gibson, September 1902, SEGC, Box 1, Folder 55.
23. Mrs. G. Rutland to Ellen Gibson, March 21, 1899, SEGC, Box 1, Folder 23.
24. Ibid.
25. Mrs. G. Rutland to Ellen Gibson, February 1, 1901, SEGC, Box 1, Folder 33.
26. Mrs. William Brunelle to Ellen Gibson, June 1901, SEGC, Box 1, Folder 37.
27. Mrs. T. W. Currie to Ellen Gibson, October 12, 1901, SEGC, Box 1, Folder 45.
28. Ellen Gibson to Mrs. Currie, October 19, 1901, SEGC, Box 1, Folder 47.
29. Ibid.
30. F. S. Osgood to Ellen Gibson, September 16, 1900, SEGC, Box 1, Folder 27, and June 14, 1901, Box 1, Folder 39.
31. Woodworth & Black to Joe Gibson, April 27, 1901, SEGC, Box 1, Folder 35.
32. Belcourt, McDougal & Smith to Ellen Gibson, September 28, 1901, SEGC, Box 1, Folder 44.
33. Rose Meder to Ellen Gibson, January 26, 1902, SEGC, Box 1, Folder 52.
34. Berton, 413. Henderson and Carmack are the Caucasian adventurers credited with discovering the gold that launched the Klondike gold rush.
35. Backhouse, 179.
36. William Lane to Ellen Gibson, June 27, 1903, SEGC, Box 1, Folder 80.
37. Robe, 165.
38. "Articles of Agreement," April 2, 1903, SEGC, Box 6, Folder 433.
39. Wickersham, 170–74.
40. Ellen Gibson to Tom and Elmer Gibson, May 8, 1903, SEGC, Box 1, Folder 69.
41. Ibid.
42. Robe, 165–69.
43. Wickersham, 212.

44. Ellen Gibson to Tom and Elmer Gibson, July 20, 1903, SEGC, Box 1, Folder 87.
45. Ellen Gibson to Tom and Elmer Gibson, June 24, 1903, SEGC, Box 1, Folder 79.
46. Ellen Gibson to Tom and Elmer Gibson, July 11, 1903, SEGC, Box 1, Folder 82.
47. Ellen Gibson to Tom and Elmer Gibson, May 26, 1903, SEGC, Box 1, Folder 71.
48. Ibid.
49. Ibid.
50. Ellen Gibson to Tom and Elmer Gibson, July 11, 1903, SEGC, Box 1, Folder 82.
51. Ellen Gibson to Tom and Elmer Gibson, May 8, 1903, SEGC, Box 1, Folder 69.
52. Ellen Gibson to Tom and Elmer Gibson, June 1, 1903, SEGC, Box 1, Folder 72.
53. Tom Gibson to Ellen Gibson, June 6, 1903, SEGC, Box 1, Folder 73.
54. Tom Gibson to Ellen Gibson, August 5, 1903, SEGC, Box 1, Folder 88.
55. Ibid.
56. Tom Gibson to Ellen Gibson, August 23, 1903, SEGC, Box 1, Folder 91.
57. Ellen Gibson to Tom Gibson, August 25, 1903, SEGC, Box 1, Folder 92.
58. Loftus, *Alaska Sportsman*, 21.
59. Tom Gibson to Ellen Gibson, July 11, 1904, SEGC, Box 2, Folder 118.
60. J. H. Tomlinson to Ellen Gibson, April 27, 1905, SEGC, Box 2, Folder 135.
61. Placer Mining Claim #8212, "Mining Locations, Fairbanks Precinct, Third Division, March 1, 1905 to May 23, 1905," Volume 5, State of Alaska Recorder's Office, Fairbanks, Alaska, 338.
62. Will Butler to Ellen Gibson, August 20, 1905, SEGC, Box 2, Folder 142.
63. Ezra W. Decoto to Ellen Gibson, February 12, 1906 and March 14, 1906, SEGC, Box 2, Folders 164 and 167.
64. Will Butler to Ellen Gibson, April 10, 1906, SEGC, Box 2, Folder 172.
65. Ellen Gibson to Tom Gibson, April 22, 1906, SEGC, Box 2, Folder 176.
66. Ellen Gibson to Tom Gibson, November 24, 1905, SEGC, Box 2, Folder 150.
67. Ellen Gibson to Mrs. DeForest, January 28, 1907, SEGC, Box 3, Folder 200; Loftus, *Alaska Magazine*, 89.
68. Mrs. John R. Hatter to Ellen Gibson, June 3, 1907, SEGC, Box 3, Folder 215.
69. Tom Gibson to Ellen Gibson, September 3, 1907, SEGC, Box 3, Folder 227.
70. Goldie Keeler to Ellen Gibson, January 12, 1908, SEGC, Box 4, Folder 277.
71. Ibid.
72. Ellen Gibson to Tom and Elmer Gibson, January 15, 1908, SEGC, Box 4, Folder 281.
73. Will Butler to Ellen Gibson, January 12, 1908, SEGC, Box 4, Folder 278.
74. "Mrs. Ellen Gibson Dead," *Fairbanks Daily Times*, May 20, 1908.
75. Quit Claim Deed from William Butler to Thomas H. Gibson, August 19, 1910, SEGC, Box 6, Folder 435.
76. Mary Jane Bell to Tom Gibson, May 1, 1911, SEGC, Box 4, Folder 360.
77. Alaska-Yukon Gazetteers, computerized database, Elmer E. Rasmuson Library, University of Alaska Fairbanks, 189.
78. 1929 United States Census, Fort Yukon Village, Circle District, Alaska, Sheet 1B.

Chapter 2

1. Aline Bradley to Walter E. Clark, April 26, 1911, Territorial Governor's Office, General Correspondence, Record Group 101, Series 130, Box 100, Folder 100–3, "Banks and Banking 1911," Alaska State Archives, Juneau, Alaska.

2. Aline Beegler's Probate File #224216, Superior Court, Los Angeles County, California; Smith College Archives, Northampton, Massachusetts; National Genealogical Society, Deceased Physician File, Arlington, Virginia; 1920 U.S. Census for Illinois and Massachusetts.

3. Thomas Neville Bonner, *To the Ends of the Earth: Women's Search for Education in Medicine* (Cambridge: Harvard University Press, 1992), 11.

4. "Register of Alumnae, Woman's Medical College of Pennsylvania," Archives and Special Collections, Hahnemann University, Philadelphia, Pennsylvania.

5. "Report on Physician's Record Search," National Genealogical Society, Deceased Physician File, Arlington, Virginia.

6. "Keen Interest in Concert," *Fairbanks Daily Times*, August 8, 1907.

7. *Fairbanks Daily Times*, August 11 and 18, 1907.

8. "In Places of Worship," *Fairbanks Sunday Times*, August 18, 1907.

9. Evangeline Atwood, *Frontier Politics: Alaska's James Wickersham* (Portland, OR: Binford & Mort, 1979), 103.

10. Meta Bloom Buttnick to author, September 8, 1998.

11. "Dr. Baskerville Dies After Long Illness" and "Great Tribute to His Memory," *Fairbanks Daily News-Miner*, September 9 and 10, 1908.

12. Meta Bloom Buttnick to author, September 8, 1998.

13. Ladies of the Presbyterian Church, *First Catch Your Moose: The Fairbanks Cookbook, 1909* (Fairbanks: Tanana-Yukon Historical Society, 1999), ix.

14. "Hospital Fair Now in Full Swing at the Auditorium," *Fairbanks Daily News-Miner*, November 9, 1910.

15. "Dr. Bradley Slighted," *Alaska Citizen*, November 23, 1914.

16. T. Cole, 124.

17. For a comprehensive history of banking in Alaska, see Terrence Cole and Elmer E. Rasmuson, *Banking on Alaska: The Story of the National Bank of Alaska* (Anchorage: National Bank of Alaska, 2000).

18. "Committee Declines to Accept Contract," *Fairbanks Weekly Times*, March 15, 1911. The committee members were E. T. Wolcott, L. N. Jesson, Aline Bradley, J. E. Robarts, W. A. Shinkle, Jesse Noble, and Thomas H. Gibson.

19. Ibid.; "Final Report by Grand Jury," *Fairbanks Weekly Times*, March 29, 1911. The following thirteen men were impaneled as jurors on February 14, 1911: George Marcus, R. T. Kubbon, Edwin C. Johnson, Ross Drennen, Robert Compton, C. J. Stewart, W. C. Harp, Charles Webb, Walter G. Fox, Arthur Thomas, N. A. Shaw, George Jestel, and John Flannagan. Due to lack of United States citizenship Marcus, Jestel, and Flannagan were excused. Shaw was appointed foreman (Foreign Corporation Docket, U.S. District Court of Alaska, Fourth Division, State Archives, Juneau, Alaska).

20. "What We Are Up Against," Editorial, *Fairbanks Weekly Times*, March 29, 1911.

21. The committee members were Aline Bradley, Kate Farrell, Mrs. J. K. Smart, Mrs. M. C. Cambridge, and Mrs. J. H. Condit, wife of the Presbyterian minister (Petition

of Depositors of Defendant in Intervention, No. 1597, District Court Fourth Division, District of Alaska, Territorial Governor's Office).

22. Aline Bradley to Walter E. Clark, April 26, 1911, Territorial Governor's Office.

23. Ibid.

24. Ibid.

25. Ibid.

26. "Our Bank Wreckers to Be Brought to Time," *Fairbanks Daily News*, May 11, 1911.

27. "Back to Help Bank Matters, Says Barnette," *Fairbanks Weekly Times*, June 26, 1911.

28. T. Cole, 136.

29. Ibid., 137.

30. "Depositors Burn Three Effigies," *Fairbanks Weekly Times*, January 13, 1913.

31. Jessie Bloom, "1974 Memoir," 55.

32. Session Laws, Resolutions and Memorials 1913 (Juneau: Daily Empire Print, 1913), 89–103; Cole and Rasmuson, 22–23.

33. Town Council Meeting Minutes, October 17, 1913, CFHR. The vote tally was: Aline Bradley 4; J. Arthur Sutherland 1; M. F. Hall 1; Melville E. Evans 0.

34. Governor J. F. A. Strong to Dr. Aline B. Bradley, January 2, 1914, Medical Board Files, State Archives, Juneau, Alaska. (Aline served with seven other physicians: H. C. DeVighne of Juneau; J. L. Myers of Ketchikan; J. H. Mustard and J. M. Sloan of Nome; J. H. Romig of Seward; Charles H. Winana of Valdez; J. Arthur Sutherland of Fairbanks.)

35. James Wickersham Diary, November 11, 1914, State Library, Juneau, Alaska.

36. Ernest Hurst Cherrington, editor, *Standard Encyclopedia of the Alcohol Problem* (Westerville, OH: n.p., 1925), 86–87.

37. James Wickersham to Governor J. F. A. Strong, Dr. Aline Bradley, and M. W. Griffith, February 2, 1917, James Wickersham Collection, Box 72, Scrapbook III, Alaska State Library, Alaska Historical Collections, Juneau, Alaska; "Prohibition Bill for Alaska Ready for Wilson's Name," *Alaska Citizen*, February 5, 1917.

38. Governor Strong to Ernest Hurst Cherrington, general manager, Anti-Saloon League of America, Westerville, Ohio, March 14, 1918, Files of the Alaska Territorial Governors, J. F. A. Strong, Microfilm Roll #55, National Archives and Records Administration, Pacific Region, Anchorage, Alaska.

39. J. F. A. Strong to Aline Bradley, September 1, 1917, J. F. A. Strong Papers, Box 1, Folder 25, Archives, Alaska and Polar Regions Department, Elmer E. Rasmuson Library, University of Alaska Fairbanks.

40. "Dr. Bradley is Admitted to Bar," *Fairbanks Daily News-Miner*, October 2, 1917; "Admission of Attorney Held Up Temporarily," *Fairbanks Daily News-Miner*, October 3, 1917.

41. Town Council Meeting Minutes, April 10, 1917, CFHR, Box 1.

42. "Almost Two to One Vote for Citizen Ticket," *Fairbanks Daily News-Miner*, April 4, 1917.

43. "Petition for Naturalization by J. F. Bradley," *Fairbanks Daily News-Miner*, October 30, 1917.

44. "Will Protest Naturalizing," *Alaska Citizen*, February 11, 1918.

45. Death Certificate for J.F. Bradley, Fairbanks Death and Birth Records, Box 1, Archives, Alaska and Polar Regions Department, Elmer E. Rasmuson Library, University of Alaska Fairbanks.

46. "In the Matter of Admission to the Bar of Aline Bradley," January 6, 1919, Attorney License Files, Alaska State Archives, Juneau, Alaska.

47. Ibid., November 8, 1920.

48. "Court Notes," *Fairbanks Daily News-Miner*, March 5, 1921.

49. Mary Zimmerman to "My dear Rachel," Harrais Family Papers (hereafter HFP), Box 1, Folder 1.

50. "Local Couple Wed Last P.M.," *Alaska Citizen*, October 23, 1919; Beegler/Bradley marriage certificate.

51. "Council Names New Magistrate," *Fairbanks Daily News-Miner*, October 4, 1922; Town Council Meeting Minutes, October 10, 1922, CFHR.

52. Jessie Bloom, "1974 Memoir," 104; "Brooks Air Trail Blazed Last Night," *Fairbanks Daily News-Miner*, July 21, 1923.

53. "Beegler Has Good Season Tolovana," *Fairbanks Daily News-Miner*, October 15, 1926.

54. "Mike Beegler Passes Away," *Fairbanks Daily News-Miner*, August 13, 1931.

55. Meta Bloom Buttnick to author, September 8, 1998.

Chapter 3

1. Bloom, "Watching Alaska Grow," 56.

2. Bloom, "1974 Memoir," 48.

3. Ibid.

4. Michael Stanislawski, *Tsar Nicholas I and the Jews: The Transformation of Jewish Society in Russia, 1825–1855* (Philadelphia: Jewish Publication Society of America, 1983), 185.

5. Steven J. Zipperstein, "Judaism in the Western Hemisphere," in *The Encyclopedia of Religion*, ed. M. Eliade (New York: Macmillan, 1987), 193.

6. J. Bloom to Jacob R. Marcus, September 30, 1962, Robert and Jessie Bloom Papers (hereafter RJBP), Archives, Alaska and Polar Regions Department, Elmer E. Rasmuson Library, University of Alaska Fairbanks, Box 5, Folder 42.

7. Matthew J. Eisenberg, "The Last Frontier: Jewish Pioneers in Alaska" (Ordination thesis, Hebrew Union College–Jewish Institute of Religion, 1991), AJAC, Box 6, Folder 59, 104.

8. J. Bloom to Jacob R. Marcus, September 30, 1962, RJBP, Box 5, Folder 42.

9. Bloom, "Fairbanks and the Ten Year Resurrection," unpublished monograph, AJAC, Box 3, Folder 23, n.p.n.

10. Bloom, Untitled monograph, AJAC, Box 3, Folder 37, 5.

11. Ibid., 6.

12. Bloom, "Watching Alaska Grow," 10.

13. Ibid.

14. Ibid., 11.

15. Ibid., 12.

16. Ibid., 13.

17. Ibid., 15.

18. Ibid., 16.
19. Ibid., 36.
20. Ibid., 41.
21. Ibid.
22. Bloom, "1974 Memoirs," 19–20.
23. Ibid., 42.
24. Ibid.
25. Ibid., 43.
26. Ibid., 13.
27. Bloom, "Watching Alaska Grow," 48.
28. Bloom, "1974 Memoir," 26.
29. Ibid., 26–27.
30. Ibid., 26.
31. Joseph Sullivan, "Sourdough Radicalism: Labor and Socialism in Alaska, 1905–1920," *Alaska History* 7: 1 (1992): 6.
32. Meta Bloom Buttnick to author, February 7, 1996; Jessie Bloom to Lena Morrow Lewis, November 9, 1949, Lena Morrow Lewis Collection, Archives, Alaska and Polar Regions Department, Elmer E. Rasmuson Library, University of Alaska Fairbanks.
33. Bloom, "1974 Memoir," 44–45.
34. Ibid., 49.
35. Ibid.
36. Ibid., 50.
37. Ibid.
38. Ibid.
39. Bloom, "Fairbanks To-Day, Yesterday and the Day Before," unpublished monograph, September 6, 1949, RJBP, Box 5, Folder 32, 1.
40. Ibid., 4.
41. Ibid., 9.
42. Bloom, "Answer to a Plea for a Honest Picture of Life in the Interior of Alaska," 1945, unpublished monograph, RJBP, Box 5, Folder 30, 6.
43. Bloom to Erica Gottfried, February 26, 1976, Oral History Collection, Manuscripts and University Archives Division, Allen Library, University of Washinton, Seattle, Washington, Tape #2.
44. Ibid.
45. "Girl is Born to the Blooms," *Fairbanks Daily News-Miner*, April 7, 1913.
46. Bloom, "1974 Memoir," 56.
47. "Big Dance is Coming Friday," *Fairbanks Daily News-Miner*, February 9, 1914.
48. "Let's Celebrate," *Fairbanks Daily News-Miner*, February 11, 1914.
49. "Fairbanksans Celebrating," *Fairbanks Daily News-Miner*, February 19, 1914.
50. Ibid.
51. "City is Preparing for a Great Celebration," *Fairbanks Daily News-Miner*, February 21, 1914.
52. Ibid.
53. Ibid.
54. "Now Come the Fireworks," *Fairbanks Daily News-Miner*, February 21, 1914.

55. "The Celebration," *Fairbanks Daily News-Miner*, February 24, 1914.
56. Bloom, "1974 Memoir," 74.
57. Ibid.
58. Advertisement, *Fairbanks Daily News-Miner*, November 16, 1918.
59. Bloom, "Contrasts," unpublished monograph, RJBP, Box 5, Folder 31, 2–3.
60. Mary Zimmerman Woods, "A brief sketch of Anna Mary Horine Zimmerman for Alaska Friends," unpublished monograph, RJBP, Box 5, Folder 39.
61. Bloom, "1974 Memoir," 67.
62. Ibid., 70–71.
63. Joe McCarthy, *Ireland* (New York: Time Inc., 1964), 63.
64. Bloom, "1974 Memoir," 78.
65. Ibid., 80.
66. Ibid., 100.
67. Ibid., 82.
68. Ibid.
69. Ibid., 85.
70. Ibid., 89.
71. Bloom, "Housekeeping in Alaska, forty years ago," unpublished monograph, RJBP, Box 5, Folder 33, n.p.n.
72. Julia Wade Abbot to Jessie Bloom, May 25, 1921, RJBP, Box 5, Folder 45.
73. Bloom, "1974 Memoir," 100.
74. Ibid., 92.
75. Bloom, "Watching Alaska Grow," 65–66.
76. Bloom, "1974 Memoir," 95.
77. Ibid., 90.
78. Eisenberg, 112.
79. Ibid., 119.
80. Ibid., 141.
81. Bloom, "History of the Fairbanks Girl Scouts," unpublished monograph, AJAC, Microfilm #193, Roll #1, 1.
82. Ibid.
83. Ibid., 5.
84. *Girl Scouts in Alaska: Spanning Six Decades, 1925–1985* (Fairbanks: Farthest North Girl Scout Council, 1985), n.p.n.
85. Eisenberg, 138.
86. J. Bloom to Jacob R. Marcus, November 18, 1962, RJBP, Box 5, Folder 42.
87. Bloom, "Watching Alaska Grow," 56.
88. Bloom to "Dear Babe and Ted," November 3, 1979.
89. Bloom to "Dear Babe and Ted," November 17, 1978.

Chapter 4

1. Margaret Keenan, "A Prayer for All Women," Women's Edition, *Fairbanks Daily News-Miner*, November 29, 1917, Harrais Family Papers (hereafter HFP), Archives, Alaska and Polar Regions Department, Elmer E. Rasmuson Library, University of Alaska Fairbanks, Box 6.

2. Margaret Keenan Harrais, "Alaska Periscope," unpublished manuscript, Valdez Public Library, Valdez, Alaska, 28.

3. "The County of Noble: Biographical Sketches," photocopy supplied by Caldwell County Library, Caldwell, Ohio, 133.

4. Ernest Hurst Cherrington, editor, *Standard Encyclopedia of the Alcohol Problem* (Westerville, OH: n.p., 1926), 1184 (courtesy of Frances E. Willard Memorial Library, Evanston, Illinois [hereafter FEWML]).

5. Harrais, Professional resume sketch, HFP, Box 1, Folder 7; Commencement Program, Northern Indiana Normal School, 1896, Archives, Valparaiso University, Valparaiso, Indiana.

6. Harrais, Professional resume sketch.

7. Harrais, "Alaska Periscope," 6.

8. Ibid., 4.

9. Ibid., 6.

10. "Idaho Marriages, 1842–1996, Custer County, Idaho, Volume 1, page 72," http://www.ancestry.com.

11. Helen D. Blair, "Margaret Keenan Harrais," article from unidentified magazine, HFP, Box 1, Folder 12.

12. Harrais, "Alaska Periscope," 27.

13. Ibid., 28.

14. Mrs. Sara Louisa Oberholtzer, "School Savings Banks," *Union Signal*, May 11, 1916, FEWML.

15. Florence Boole, "WCTU Convention in the Northland," *Union Signal*, October 5, 1916, FEWML.

16. "Program of First Territorial Convention Woman's Christian Temperance Union," *Daily Alaskan* (Skagway), May 13, 1915.

17. "Miss Keenan Elected Head of Schools," *Fairbanks Daily News-Miner*, July 14, 1916; Fairbanks School Board to Margaret Keenan, July 11, 1916, HFP, Box 1, Folder 7.

18. Cornelia T. Hatcher, "Campaigning in the Heart of Alaska," *Union Signal*, September 28, 1916, FEWML.

19. "Mrs. Hatcher Ends Prohibition Fight," *Fairbanks Daily News-Miner*, July 13, 1916.

20. Hatcher, "Campaigning in the Heart of Alaska."

21. "Mrs. Hatcher Ends Prohibition Fight."

22. Harrais, "Alaska Periscope," 126.

23. Ruth Bordin, *Woman and Temperance: The Quest for Power and Liberty, 1873–1900* (Philadelphia: Temple University Press, 1981), xiv and xvi.

24. "Reception is Given for Miss Keenan," *Fairbanks Daily News-Miner*, November 7, 1916.

25. "Vice-President of Alaska WCTU Visits National Headquarters," *Union Signal*, July 12–19, 1917, FEWML.

26. Niilo E. Koponen, "The History of Education in Alaska: With Special Reference to the Relationship Between the Bureau of Indian Affairs Schools and the State School System" (EdD thesis, Harvard University, 1964), 24.

27. Ibid., 34.

28. Prohibition of Liquors in Territory of Alaska, HR 19188, 64th Cong., 2nd sess., 1917, 25.

29. Prohibition in Alaska, S 7963, 64th Cong., 2nd sess., 1917, 9.

30. William K. Keller, "A History of Education in Alaska 1741–1940" (EdD thesis, State College of Washington, 1940), 116–20.
31. "Vice-President of Alaska WCTU Visits National Headquarters," *Union Signal*, July 12–19, 1917, FEWML.
32. Harrais, "Alaska Periscope," 43.
33. Ibid., 42.
34. Ibid., 46.
35. Ibid., 56.
36. Ibid.
37. Ibid., 65.
38. Women's Edition, *Fairbanks Daily News-Miner*, November 29, 1917, HFP, Box 6.
39. Harrais, "Alaska Periscope," 67.
40. Mary Lee Davis probably complained about the spelling of her name, which appeared in print as "Mary Lea Davis."
41. Harrais, "Alaska Periscope," 73.
42. Ibid., 74.
43. Ibid., 73.
44. Report of War Work of Fairbanks, Alaska Public School, HFP, Box 1, Folder 8.
45. Harrais, "Alaska Periscope," 77.
46. John Butrovitch, interview with author, September 28, 1995.
47. Harrais, "Alaska Periscope," 80.
48. Ibid., 91c.
49. Ibid., 93.
50. Mary H. Zimmerman to Margaret Keenan, March 1, 1917, HFP, Box 1, Folder 7.
51. Harrais, "Alaska Periscope," 112.
52. Ibid., 108.
53. Ibid., 118.
54. Ibid., 122.
55. Ibid., 124.
56. Ibid., 153.
57. Ibid., 172.
58. Ibid., 185.
59. Ibid., 191.
60. Ibid., 190.
61. Ibid., 194.
62. Obituary, Martin Luther Harrais, *Valdez Miner*, HFP, Box 3, Folder 2.
63. Margarite (unidentified surname) to Margaret Keenan Harrais, September 18, 1932, HFP, Box 2, Folder 3.
64. Ibid.
65. Ibid.
66. Jeannette P. Nichols to Margaret Keenan Harrais, August 20, 1941, HFP, Box 2, Folder 3.
67. Anita Diamant to Margaret Keenan Harrais, June 3, 1943, HFP, Box 2, Folder 3.
68. Margaret Keenan Harrais to Anita Diamant, August 2, 1943, HFP, Box 2, Folder 3.
69. "Tribute to an Alaska Lady," Congressional Record—Senate, September 6, 1962, HFP, Box 3, Folder 2.

70. Edby Davis to Margaret Keenan Harrais, December 11, 1946, HFP, Box 1, Folder 1.

71. Margaret Keenan Harrais to Dora M. Sweeney, February 6, 1952, HFP, Box 2, Folder 3.

72. "Tribute to an Alaska Lady."

73. Mrs. G. W. Lamson to "To Whom It May Concern," July 18, 1914, HFP, Box 1, Folder 7.

74. This unfinished afghan is part of the Dorothy Clifton Collection in the Archives at the University of Alaska Fairbanks.

75. Agnes Dubbs Hays, *Heritage of Dedication: One Hundred Years of the National Woman's Christian Temperance Union 1874–1974* (Evanston, IL: Signal Press, 1973), 139.

Chapter 5

1. Mary Lee Davis, *Uncle Sam's Attic: The Intimate Story of Alaska* (Boston: W. A. Wilde Company, 1930), 118.

2. *Descriptive of Fairbanks, "Alaska's Golden Heart"* (Fairbanks: The Fairbanks Commercial Club, April 1916), 7.

3. Ibid., 5.

4. In 1916, it was estimated that the Fairbanks community required 18,500 cords of wood per year to furnish heat and electricity (George Watkin Evans, "Report on the Lignite Creek Coal Area, Nenana Coal Mining District, Alaska," November 22, 1916, 24).

5. Newton Woodworth Cadwell, biographical notes, Alumnae Files, Hamilton College, Clinton, New York (hereafter Hamilton College).

6. Mary Lee Davis, "Little Sister," *Wellesley Magazine* (December 1905), 102.

7. Ibid.

8. Ibid., 109.

9. Estelle Clark Harris, "Mrs. Cadwell, The Ideal Minister's Wife, Her Twenty Years in Westfield" (article about a talk given by Harris on October 11, 1915, the occasion of the unveiling of the bronze tablet in honor of Jane Cadwell, Olivet Presbyterian Church, Atlantic City, New Jersey), courtesy of Hamilton College.

10. Obituary, Jane Worrall Criswell Cadwell, *Atlantic City Daily Press*, July 4, 1914, Atlantic City Free Public Library, Atlantic City, New Jersey.

11. Harris.

12. Ibid.

13. *International Genealogical Index, 2001 Edition*, Family History Library, Church of Jesus Christ of Latter-day Saints, Salt Lake City, Utah.

14. "Notable Resident Dies, Hospitalized 5 Years," *Inquirer and Mirror* (Nantucket, Massachusetts), January 27, 1966, Nantucket Historical Society, Nantucket, Massachusetts.

15. Mary Lee Cadwell Davis, Application, National Society Daughters of the American Revolution, Washington, D.C., and Alaska Chapter, National Society Daughters of the American Revolution, Fairbanks, Alaska, "Yearbook 1999–2000," n.p., n.d., 11.

16. Davis, *Uncle Sam's Attic*, 23.

17. Ibid.

18. Newton Woodworth Cadwell, autobiographical sketch, May 29, 1916, Hamilton College.

19. "Radcliffe Alumnae Information, 1928," Radcliffe College.

20. Meta Bloom Buttnick to author, April 26, 1996.

21. "Radcliffe Alumnae Information, 1928," Radcliffe College.

22. Meta Bloom Buttnick to author, January 16, 1996; Elizabeth Andrews, archivist, to author, February 29, 1996, Institute Archives and Special Collections, Massachusetts Institute of Technology, Cambridge, Massachusetts.

23. Mary Lee Davis, "On the Ute Trail," *Wellesley Magazine*, June 1910, 377.

24. Ibid., 390.

25. Sumner S. Smith, *The Mining Industry in the Territory of Alaska During the Calendar Year 1916*, Department of the Interior, Bulletin 153 (Washington, D.C.: Government Printing Office, 1917), 8.

26. "Davis Here to Open Station," *Fairbanks Daily News-Miner*, July 16, 1917.

27. Davis, *Uncle Sam's Attic*, 103–4.

28. Mary Lea [*sic*] Davis, "The Man Behind the Pick," Women's Edition, *Fairbanks Daily News-Miner*, November 29, 1917, HFP, Box 6.

29. Walter Lowrie Fisher, Secretary of the Interior, "Address on Alaskan Problems," Before the American Mining Congress at Chicago, Illinois, October 27, 1911 (Washington, D.C., 1911), 4.

30. Davis, *Uncle Sam's Attic*, 70 and 91.

31. Ibid., 300.

32. Murphy and Haigh, 11.

33. Davis, *Uncle Sam's Attic*, 334.

34. Ibid., 143.

35. Mary Lee Davis, "God's Pocket," *Scribner's* magazine, June 1924, 660.

36. Mary Lee Davis, "Who Lives in Alaska—And Why?," *Scribner's* magazine, May 1929, 576.

37. Ibid., 577.

38. Mary Lee Davis, *We Are Alaskans* (Boston: W. A. Wilde Company, 1931), 119.

39. Ibid.

40. Ibid., 5.

41. Jessie Bloom, "1974 Memoir," 89.

42. Griese and Bigelow, 5.

43. Ibid., 22–26.

44. Meta Bloom Buttnick to author, January 16, 1996.

45. Mary Lee Davis, "Uncle Sam and the Treasure of the Humble," *Alaskan Churchman*, February 1919, 46–47.

46. "Who Will Sew for Refugees?" *Fairbanks Daily News-Miner*, October 30, 1918.

47. *Fairbanks Daily News-Miner*, April 8, 1920.

48. Ibid., April 26, 1920.

49. Unnamed Bostrom, certificate of birth, Fairbanks Death and Birth Records, Archives, Alaska and Polar Regions Department, Elmer E. Rasmuson Library, University of Alaska Fairbanks.

50. Davis, *We Are Alaskans*, 285–311.

51. *Fairbanks Daily News-Miner*, June 28, 1920.

52. Janet Matheson, *Fairbanks: A City Historic Building Survey* (City of Fairbanks, 1978), n.p.n.

53. National Register of Historic Places Inventory—Nomination Form, Fairbanks North Star Borough, Fairbanks, Alaska.

54. Smith, 8.

55. Davis, *We Are Alaskans*, 182 and 198.

56. Davis, *Uncle Sam's Attic*, 202.

57. Ibid., 203–4.

58. "Who Are the Alaskans?" *Boston Herald*, July 25, 1931, Joyce Cadwell Lewis Personal Collection.

59. Frank G. Carpenter, *Alaska: Our Northern Wonderland* (New York: Doubleday, Page & Company, 1923), 282.

60. Davis, *We Are Alaskans*, 181.

61. Carpenter, photo caption facing 100; Davis, *We Are Alaskans*, 185.

62. Davis, *We Are Alaskans*, 188.

63. Davis, *Uncle Sam's Attic*, 159.

64. Ibid., 161.

65. Davis, *We Are Alaskans*, 59.

66. "Bill of Sale," John Reeves Personal Collection.

67. "Davis' Leave for Outside," *Fairbanks Daily News-Miner*, October 17, 1924.

68. Ibid.; Dan Sutherland to W. A. Wilde Publishing Co., May 5, 1930, Wellesley College; Allan H. Wilde to Eunice Lathrope, October 8, 1930, Wellesley College.

69. Biographical sketch of Mary Lee Davis, Wellesley College.

70. Michael J. Kippenbrock, *Alaskan Churchman* (October 1930), 119.

71. Melvin B. Ricks, *A Basic Bibliography of Alaskan Literature, Annotated* (Juneau: 1960), Alaska State Library, Alaska Historical Collections, Juneau, Alaska, 101.

72. Newspaper clipping, *Boston Herald*, March 21, 1931; "Alumnae Update Information, 1931," Wellesley College.

73. Ricks, 102.

74. "New Books at Random," *Evening Star* (Washington, D.C.), August 11, 1931; "Who Are the Alaskans?" *Boston Herald*, July 20, 1931, Joyce Cadwell Lewis Personal Collection.

75. Promotional brochure, *Sourdough Gold: The Log of a Yukon Adventure*, Wellesley College.

76. Ibid.

77. "Vice-President's Lady," *Good Housekeeping*, March 1929; "Precedence and Precedents," *Ladies' Home Journal*, August 1929.

78. Meta Bloom Buttnick to author, April 16, 1996; Joyce Cadwell Lewis to author, May 7, 1996.

79. Paul N. Cadwell to Mr. Love, October 30, 1950, Hamilton College.

80. "1906," *Wellesley Alumnae Magazine*, October 1950, 44.

81. Ibid.

82. Obituaries for John Allen Davis from unidentified newspaper, August 31, 1962; Mary Lee Davis, Nantucket Atheneum (Nantucket, Massachusetts), January 27, 1966.

83. *Fairbanks Daily News-Miner*, July 29, 1931.

84. Ibid.

85. *Fairbanks Daily News-Miner*, July 30, 1931.

86. Ibid.

Conclusion

1. "Pioneer Women of Northland," unidentified newspaper article, Member's Recollections, Pioneer Women of Alaska, RFP.
2. David Richardson, James Geoghegan Collection finding aid, Archives, Alaska and Polar Regions Department, Elmer E. Rasmuson Library, University of Alaska Fairbanks.
3. Harrais, "Alaska Periscope," 28.
4. Sandra L. Myres, *Westering Women and the Frontier Experience, 1800–1915* (Albuquerque: University of New Mexico Press, 1982), 14.
5. Ibid.
6. Ibid., 139.
7. Ibid., 146.
8. Cathy Luchetti and Carol Olwell, *Women of the West*, Library of the American West, ed. Herman J. Viola (New York: Crown Trade Paperbacks, 1982), 28–9.
9. Myres, 185.
10. Ibid., 205.
11. Ibid., 213.
12. Ibid., 209.
13. Ibid., 238.
14. Ibid., 185 and 246.
15. Bill McKibben, *The End of Nature* (New York: Anchor Books/Doubleday, 1989), 8.

Bibliography

Archival Materials

Alaska State Archives, Juneau, Alaska
    Territorial Governor's Office Collection
    Medical Board Files
    Attorney License Files
Alaska State Library, Juneau, Alaska
    James Wickersham Collection
Atlantic City Free Public Library, Atlantic City, New Jersey
Caldwell County Library, Caldwell, Ohio
Dawson City Museum and Historical Society, Dawson City, Yukon Territory, Canada
Frances E. Willard Memorial Library, Evanston, Illinois
Genealogical Society of the West Fields, Westfield, New Jersey
Hahnemann University, Archives and Special Collections, Philadelphia, Pennsylvania
Hamilton College, Clinton, New York
Nantucket Athenaeum, Nantucket, Massachusetts
Nantucket Historical Society, Nantucket, Massachusetts
National Archives and Records Administration, Pacific Region, Anchorage, Alaska
    Files of the Alaska Territorial Governors
National Genealogical Society, Arlington, Virginia
Princeton University, Princeton, New Jersey, Seeley G. Mudd Manuscript Library
Radcliffe College, Cambridge, Massachusetts, Archives, The Arthur and Elizabeth Schlesinger Library
Smith College, Northampton, Massachusetts, Archives
University of Alaska Fairbanks, Fairbanks, Alaska, Archives, Alaska and Polar Regions Department:
        Alaska Nurses' Association Collection
        American Jewish Archives Collection
        Gaustad Bartlett Collection
        Robert and Jessie Bloom Papers
        City of Fairbanks Historical Records
        Fairbanks Death and Birth Records
        John A. Clark Papers
        Dorothy Clifton Collection
        Dr. G. W. Gasser Collection
        James Geoghegan Collection
        Sarah Ellen Gibson Collection
        Harrais Family Papers

Lena Morrow Lewis Collection
MacKay Collection
Rust Family Papers
Skinner Vertical File
J. F. A. Strong Papers
James M. Whitely Collection
Valdez Public Library, Valdez, Alaska
Valparaiso University, Valparaiso, Indiana
Wellesley College, Wellesley, Massachusetts, Archives, Margaret Clapp Library
Wilson College, Chambersburg, Pennsylvania, C. Elizabeth Boyd Archival Center
Eisenberg, Matthew J. "The Last Frontier: Jewish Pioneers in Alaska." Ordination thesis, Hebrew Union College–Jewish Institute of Religion, 1991.
Keller, William K. "A History of Education in Alaska 1741–1940." EdD thesis, State College of Washington, 1940.
Koponen, Niilo E. "The History of Education in Alaska: With Special Reference to the Relationship Between the Bureau of Indian Affairs Schools and the State School System." EdD thesis, Harvard University, 1964.
Muckenthaller, Stella. "The Inception and Early Development Years of St. Joseph Hospital, Fairbanks, Alaska." Master's thesis, Catholic University of America, 1967.
Robe, Cecil Francis. "The Penetration of an Alaskan Frontier: The Tanana Valley and Fairbanks." PhD diss., Yale University, 1943.

Books

Atwood, Evangeline. *Frontier Politics: Alaska's James Wickersham*. Portland, OR: Binford & Mort, 1979.
Backhouse, Frances. *Women of the Klondike*. Vancouver/Toronto: Whitecap Books, 1995.
Berton, Pierre. *The Klondike Fever*. New York: Alfred A. Knopf, 1958.
Bonner, Thomas Neville. *To the Ends of the Earth: Women's Search for Education in Medicine*. Cambridge, MA: Harvard University Press, 1992.
Bordin, Ruth. *Woman and Temperance: The Quest for Power and Liberty, 1873–1900*. Philadelphia: Temple University Press, 1981.
Bowman, Isaiah. *The Pioneer Fringe*. New York: American Geographical Society, 1931.
Carpenter, Frank G. *Alaska: Our Northern Wonderland*. New York: Doubleday, Page & Company, 1923.
Cherrington, Ernest Hurst, ed. *Standard Encyclopedia of the Alcohol Problem*. Westerville, OH: 1925.
Cole, Dermot. *Fairbanks: A Gold Rush Town That Beat the Odds*. Fairbanks/Seattle: Epicenter Press, 1999.
Cole, Terrence. *E. T. Barnette: The Strange Story of the Man Who Founded Fairbanks*. Anchorage: Alaska Northwest Publishing Company, 1981.
Cole, Terrence, and Elmer E. Rasmuson. *Banking on Alaska: The Story of the National Bank of Alaska*. Anchorage: National Bank of Alaska, 2000. Available from the University of Alaska Press, Fairbanks.
Davis, Mary Lee. *Uncle Sam's Attic: The Intimate Story of Alaska*. Boston: W. A. Wilde Company, 1930.
————. *We Are Alaskans*. Boston: W. A. Wilde Company, 1931.

Ducker, James H. *Carmack's Alaskans: A Census Study of Alaskans in 1900*. Alaska Historical Commission, 1983.

Fairbanks Chamber of Commerce. *Tanana Valley Alaska*. Seattle: Metropolitan Press Printing Co., n.d.

Furnas, J.C. *The Americans: A Social History of the United States 1587–1914*. New York: G.P. Putnam's Sons, 1969.

Girl Scouts in Alaska: Spanning Six Decades, 1925–1985. Fairbanks: Farthest North Girl Scout Council, 1985.

Griese, Arnold, and Ed Bigelow. *O Ye Frost and Cold: The History of St. Matthew's Church, Fairbanks, Alaska*. Fairbanks: St. Matthew's Episcopal Church, 1980.

Haycox, Stephen. *Alaska: An American Colony*. Seattle: University of Washington Press, 2002.

Hays, Agnes Dubbs. *Heritage of Dedication: One Hundred Years of the National Woman's Christian Temperance Union 1874–1974*. Evanston, IL: Signal Press, 1973.

Ladies of the Presbyterian Church, compilers. *First Catch Your Moose: The Fairbanks Cook Book, 1909*. Reprint, Fairbanks: Tanana-Yukon Historical Society, 1999.

Lautaret, Ronald. *Alaskan Historical Documents Since 1867*. Jefferson, NC, and London: McFarland & Company, 1989.

Luchetti, Cathy, and Carol Olwell. *Women of the West*. New York: Crown Trade Paperbacks, 1982.

Matheson, Janet. *Fairbanks: A City Historic Building Survey*. City of Fairbanks, 1978.

May, Ernest T. *War, Boom and Bust: The Life History of the United States, Volume 10: 1917–1932*. New York: Time Inc., 1964.

Mayer, Melanie J. *Klondike Women: True Tales of the 1897–1898 Gold Rush*. Athens, OH: Swallow Press/Ohio University Press, 1989.

McCarthy, Joe. *Ireland*. New York: Time Inc., 1964.

McKibben, Bill. *The End of Nature*. New York: Anchor Books/Doubleday, 1989.

Murie, Margaret E. *Two in the Far North*. New York: Alfred A. Knopf, 1962.

Murphy, Claire Rudolf, and Jane G. Haigh. *Gold Rush Women*. Anchorage: Alaska Northwest Books, 1997.

Myres, Sandra L. *Westering Women and the Frontier Experience 1800–1915*. Albuquerque: University of New Mexico Press, 1982.

Nevin, Alfred. *Centennial Biography: Men of Mark of Cumberland Valley Pennsylvania 1776–1876*. Philadelphia: Fulton Publishing Company, 1876.

Ricks, Melvin B. *A Basic Bibliography of Alaskan Literature, Annotated*. Juneau: By the author, 1960.

Rollins, Alden M., compiler. *Census Alaska: Numbers of Inhabitants, 1792–1970*. Anchorage: University of Alaska Anchorage Library, 1978.

Session Laws, Resolutions and Memorials 1913. Juneau: Daily Empire Print, 1913.

Stanislawski, Michael. *Tsar Nicholas I and the Jews: The Transformation of Jewish Society in Russia, 1825–1855*. Philadelphia: Jewish Publication Society of America, 1983.

Tanana Directory, 1907. N.p., n.d.

Wade, Richard C. *The Urban Frontier: The Rise of Western Cities, 1790–1830*. Cambridge, MA: Harvard University Press, 1959.

West, Elliott. "Beyond Baby Doe: Child Rearing on the Mining Frontier." In *The Women's West*, edited by Susan Armitage and Elizabeth Jameson. Norman: University of Oklahoma Press, 1987.

Wickersham, James. *Old Yukon: Tales—Trails—and Trials.* Washington, D.C.: Washington Law Book Co., 1938. Edited and annotated edition, Fairbanks: University of Alaska Press, 2009.

Wold, Jo Anne. *This Old House: The Story of Clara Rust, Alaska Pioneer.* Anchorage: Alaska Northwest Publishing Company, 1976.

Zipperstein, Steven J. "Judaism in the Western Hemisphere." In *The Encyclopedia of Religion*, edited by M. Eliade. New York: Macmillan, 1987.

Pamphlets

Descriptive of Fairbanks, "Alaska's Golden Heart." Fairbanks: The Fairbanks Commercial Club, 1916.

Tanana Valley Alaska. Seattle: Metropolitan Press Printing Co.

"Yearbook 1999–2000." Fairbanks, Alaska Chapter, Daughters of the American Revolution, n.d.

Government Publications

Bureau of Vital Statistics, Department of Health and Social Services, Juneau, Alaska.

Evans, George Watkin. "Report on the Lignite Creek Coal Area, Nenana Coal Mining District, Alaska." 1916.

Fairbanks North Star Borough, Fairbanks, Alaska. "National Register of Historic Places Inventory."

Fisher, Walter Lowrie, Secretary of the Interior. Address on Alaskan Problems, Before the American Mining Congress at Chicago, Illinois, October 27, 1911. Washington, D.C., 1911.

Smith, Sumner S. *The Mining Industry in the Territory of Alaska During the Calendar Year 1916*, Department of the Interior, Bulletin 153. Washington, D.C.: Government Printing Office, 1917.

State of Alaska Recorder's Office. "Mining Locations, Fairbanks Precinct, Third Division, March 1, 1905 to May 23, 1905," Volume 5.

Superior Court, Los Angeles County, California.

United States Census Records.

U.S. Congress. House. Conditions in Alaska, Hearings, House of Representatives, 1912. Washington, D.C.: Government Printing Office, 1912.

U.S. Congress. House. Prohibition of Liquors in Territory of Alaska. HR 19188. 64th Cong., 2nd sess., 1917.

U.S. Congress. Senate. Prohibition in Alaska. S 7963. 64th Cong., 2nd sess., 1917.

Periodicals

Alaska History, 1992

Alaska Magazine, 1977

Alaska Sportsman, 1967

Alaskan Churchman, 1907, 1919, and 1930

Good Housekeeping, 1929

Ladies' Home Journal, 1929

Pathfinder of Alaska, 1921

Scribner's magazine, 1924 and 1929

Wellesley Magazine, 1905 and 1910

Newspapers

Alaska Citizen (Fairbanks), 1914–1919
Daily Alaska Dispatch (Juneau), 1912
Daily Alaskan (Skagway), 1915
Fairbanks Daily News, 1911
Fairbanks Daily News-Miner, 1908–1973
Fairbanks Daily Times, 1907 and 1908
Fairbanks Sunday Times, 1907
Fairbanks News, "The Tanana Gold Fields," 1904
Fairbanks Weekly Times, 1911 and 1913
Valdez Miner, 1935

Computerized Information Service

Alaska-Yukon Gazetteers, Elmer E. Rasmuson Library, University of Alaska Fairbanks
Ancestry.com
H-Net Humanities & Social Sciences OnLine
International Genealogical Index, 2001 Edition, Family History Library, Church of Jesus
    Christ of Latter-day Saints, Salt Lake City

Correspondence

Ackerman, Kay. C. Elizabeth Boyd Archival Center, Wilson College, Chambersburg,
    Pennsylvania.
Andrews, Elizabeth. Institute Archives and Special Collections, Massachusetts Institute of
    Technology, Boston, Massachusetts.
Buttnick, Meta Bloom. Seattle, Washington.
Hansen, Phyllis. Genealogical Society of the West Fields, Westfield, New Jersey.
Kelker, Signe. Special Collections, Ezra Lehman Memorial Library, Shippensburg
    University, Shippensburg, Pennsylvania.
Lewis, Joyce Cadwell, Kuttawa, Kentucky.

Organization Applications

Davis, Mary Lee Cadwell, Daughters of the American Revolution, Washington, D.C.
National number 202073.

Oral Histories

Bloom, Jessie with Erica Gottfried, February 1976. Special Collections, Allen Library,
    University of Washington, Seattle.
Butrovitch, John with author, September 1995. Author's personal collection.

Personal Collections

Joyce Cadwell Lewis, Kuttawa, Kentucky
John Reeves, Fairbanks, Alaska
Candace Waugaman, Fairbanks, Alaska

Index

Note: Italicized page numbers indicate photographs or figures.

Z